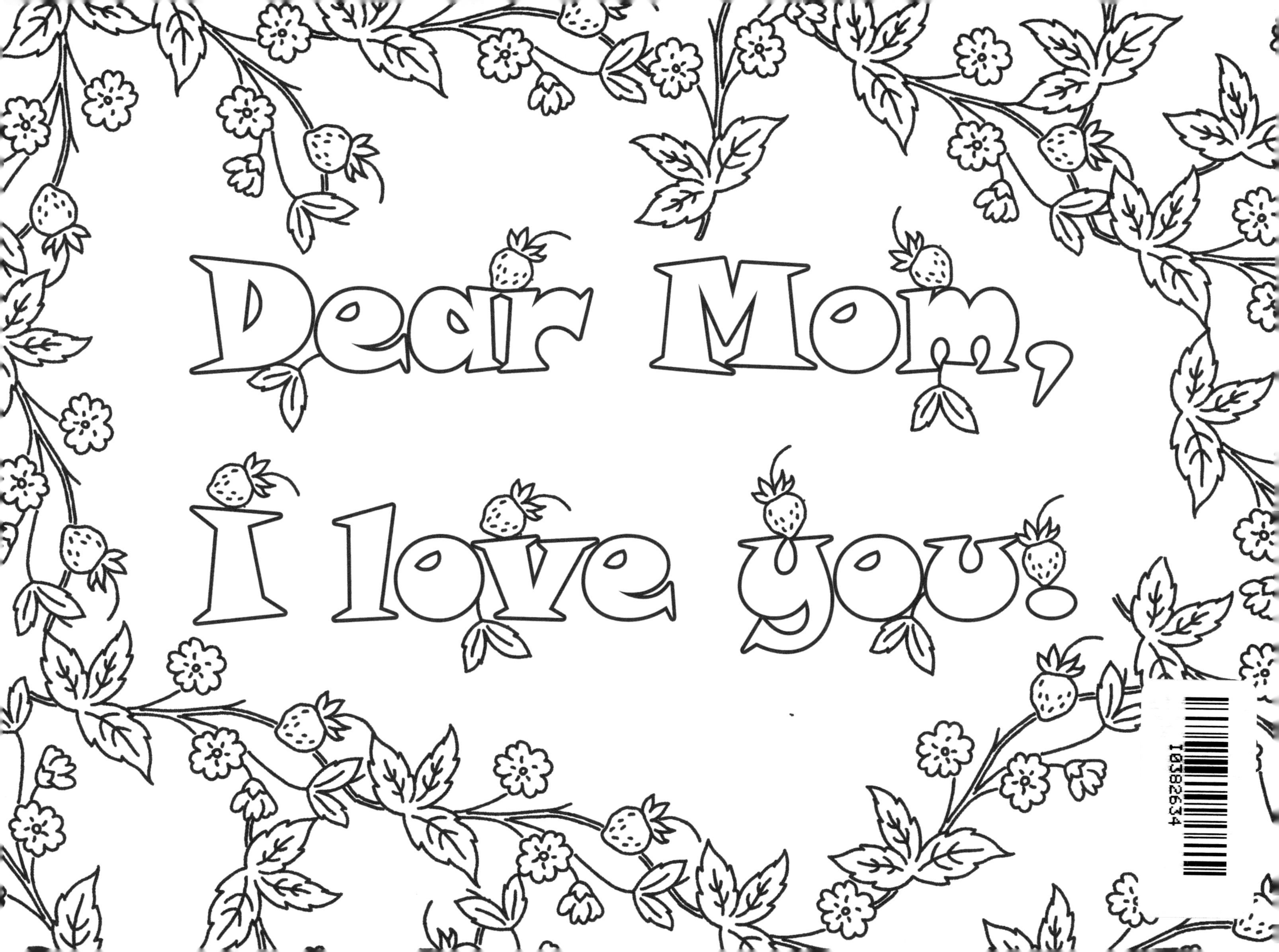

10382634

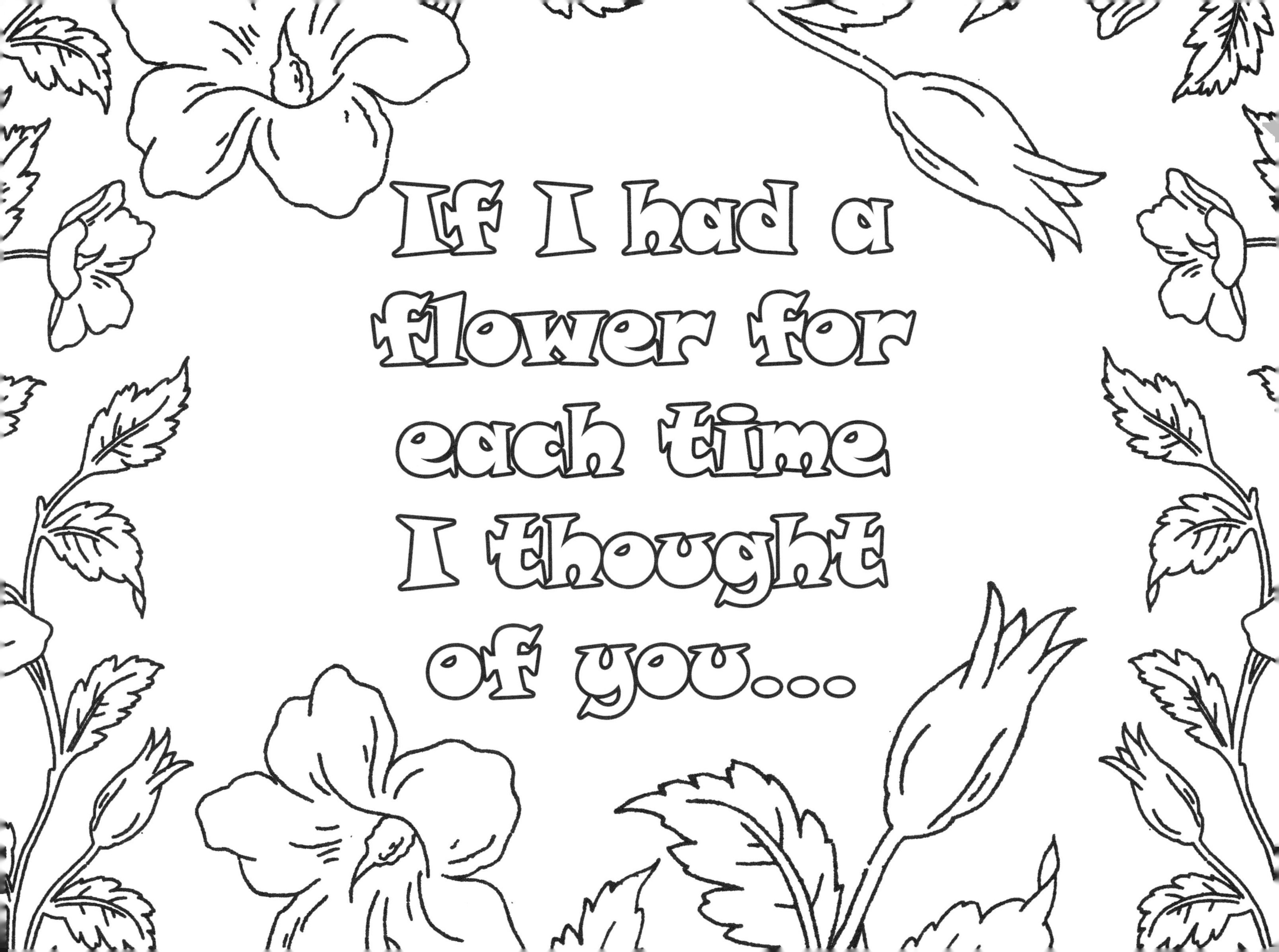
If I had a
flower for
each time
I thought
of you...

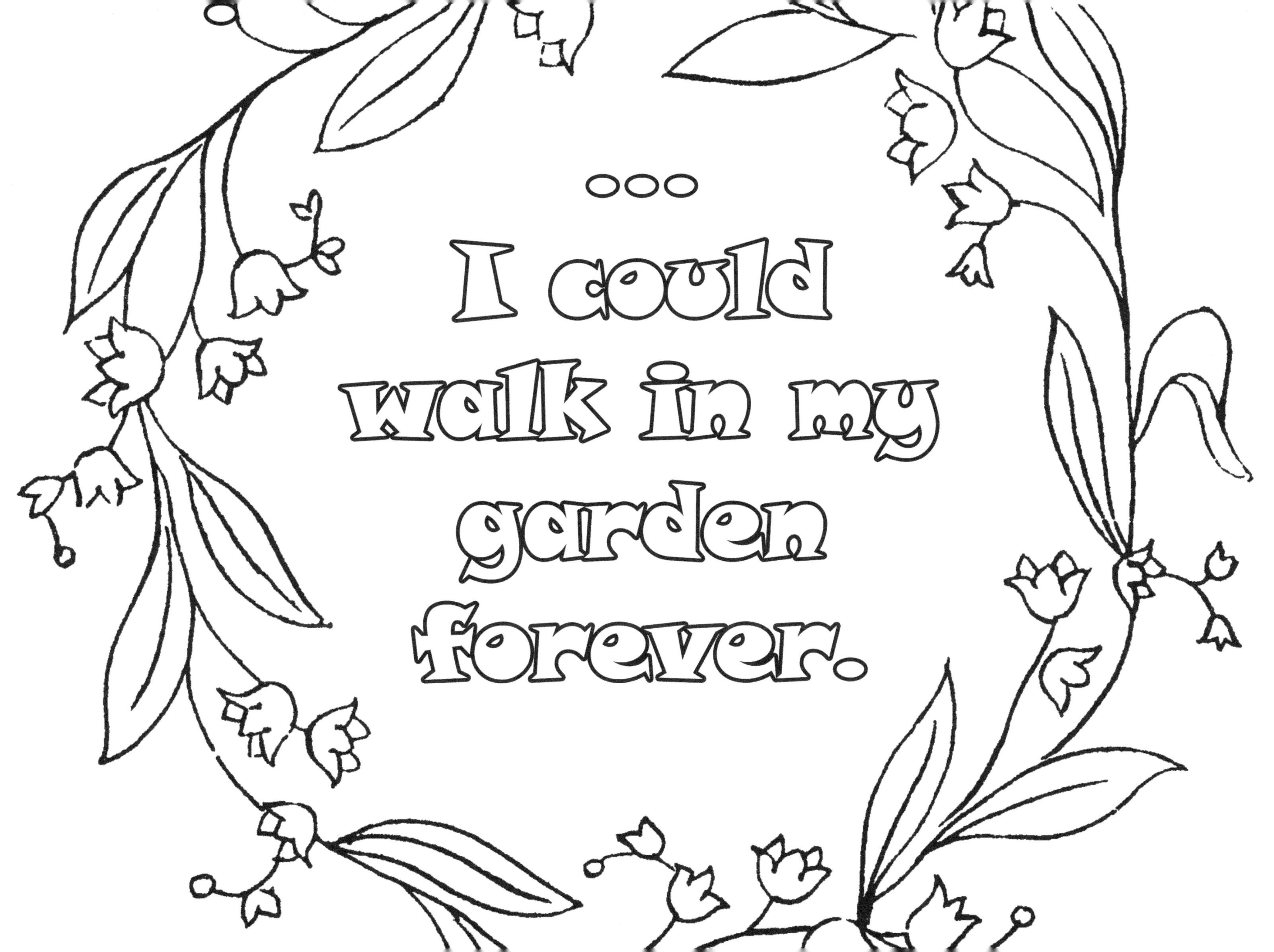
...
I could
walk in my
garden
forever.

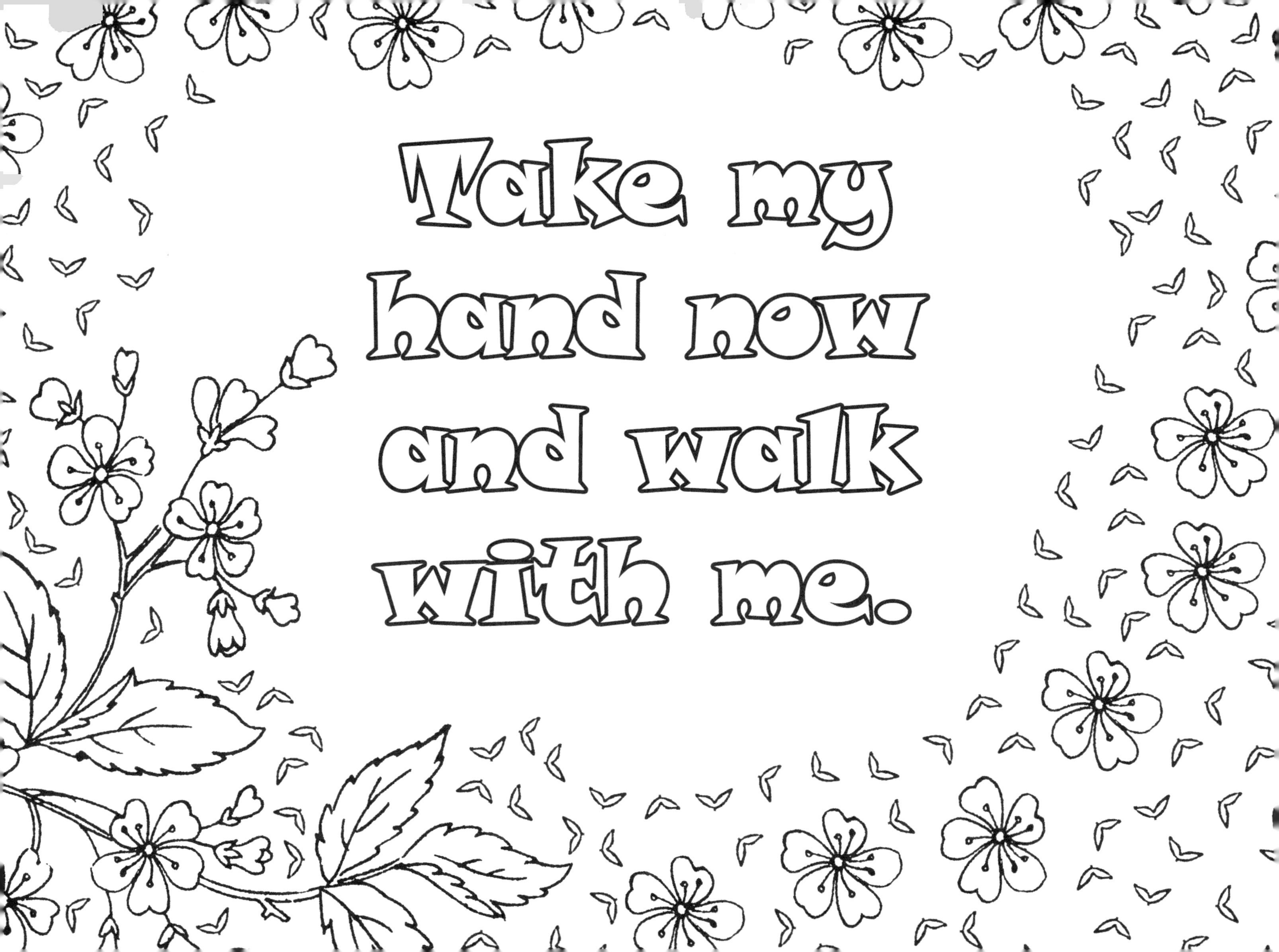
Take my hand now and walk with me.

Mothers hold their children's hands for a short while, but their hearts forever.

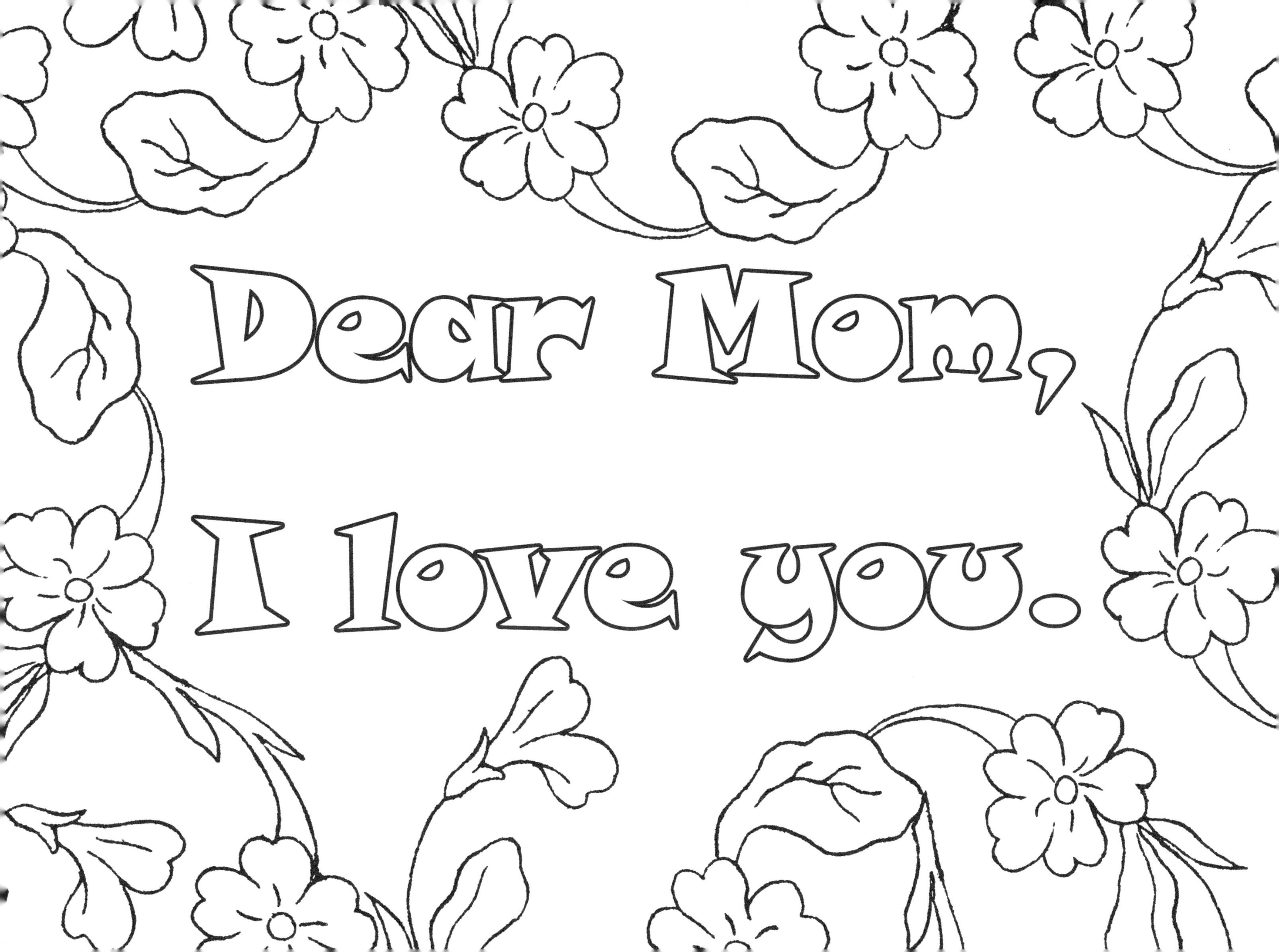
Dear Mom,
I love you.

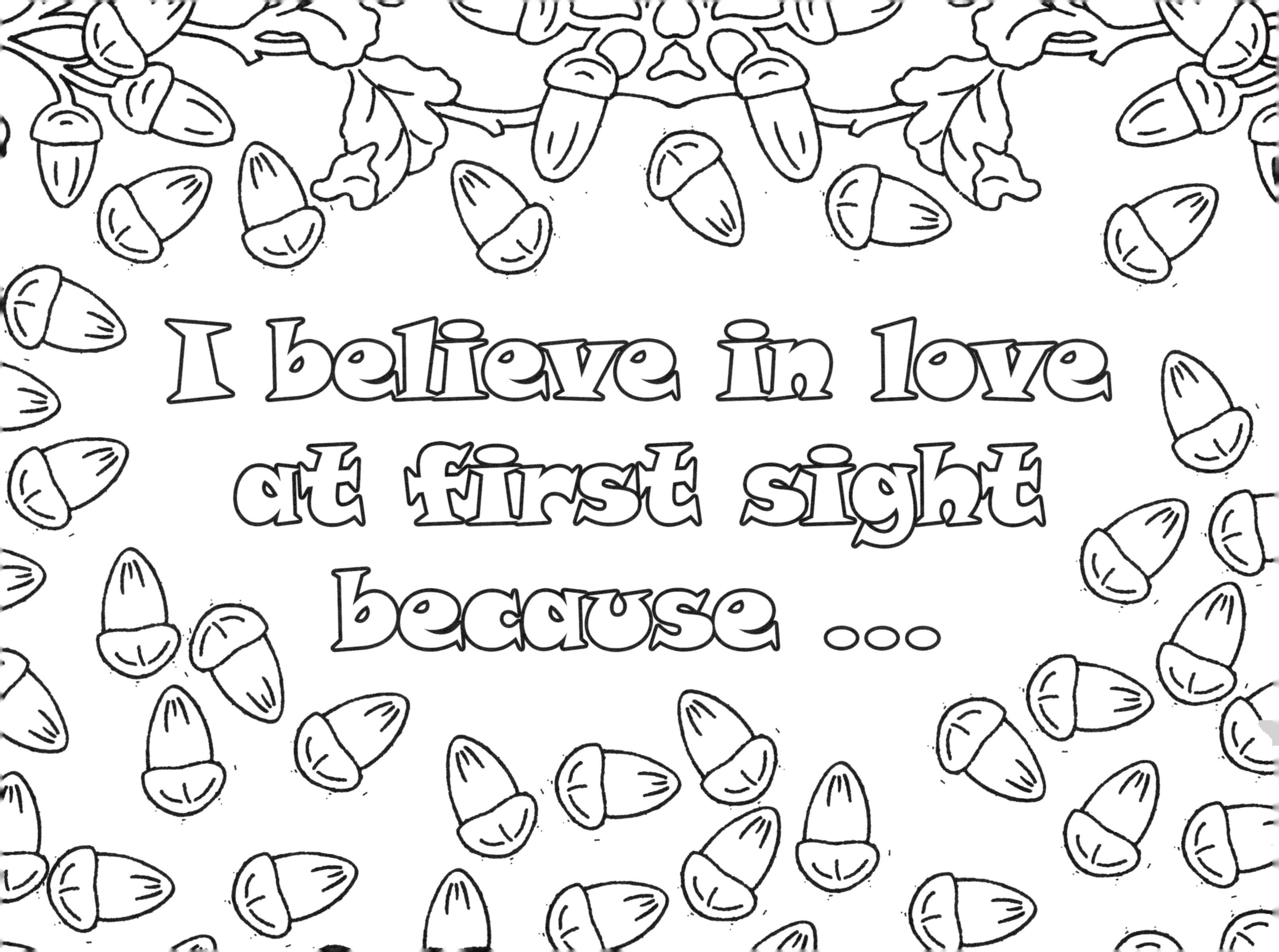
I believe in love
at first sight
because ...

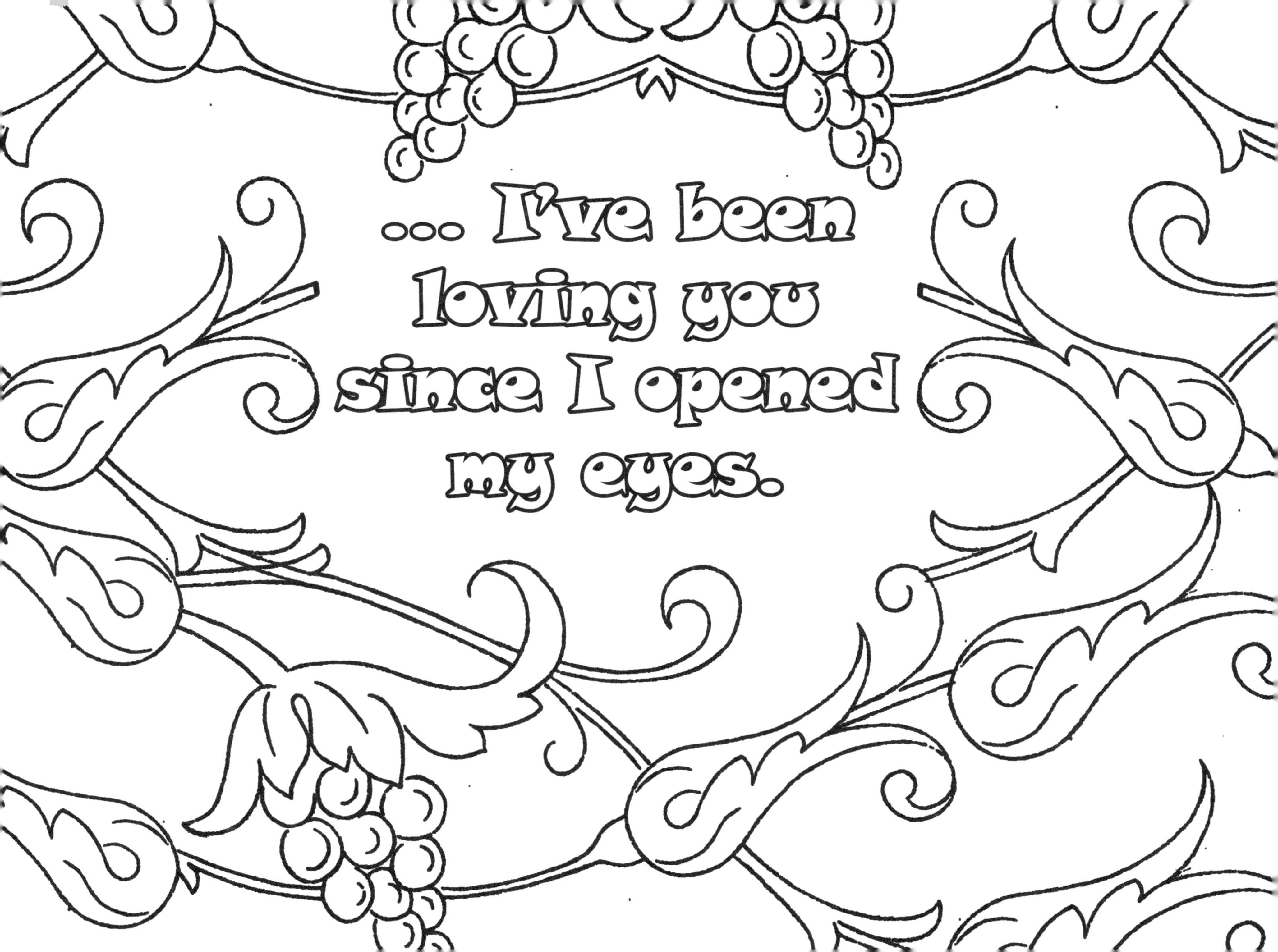
... I've been
loving you
since I opened
my eyes.

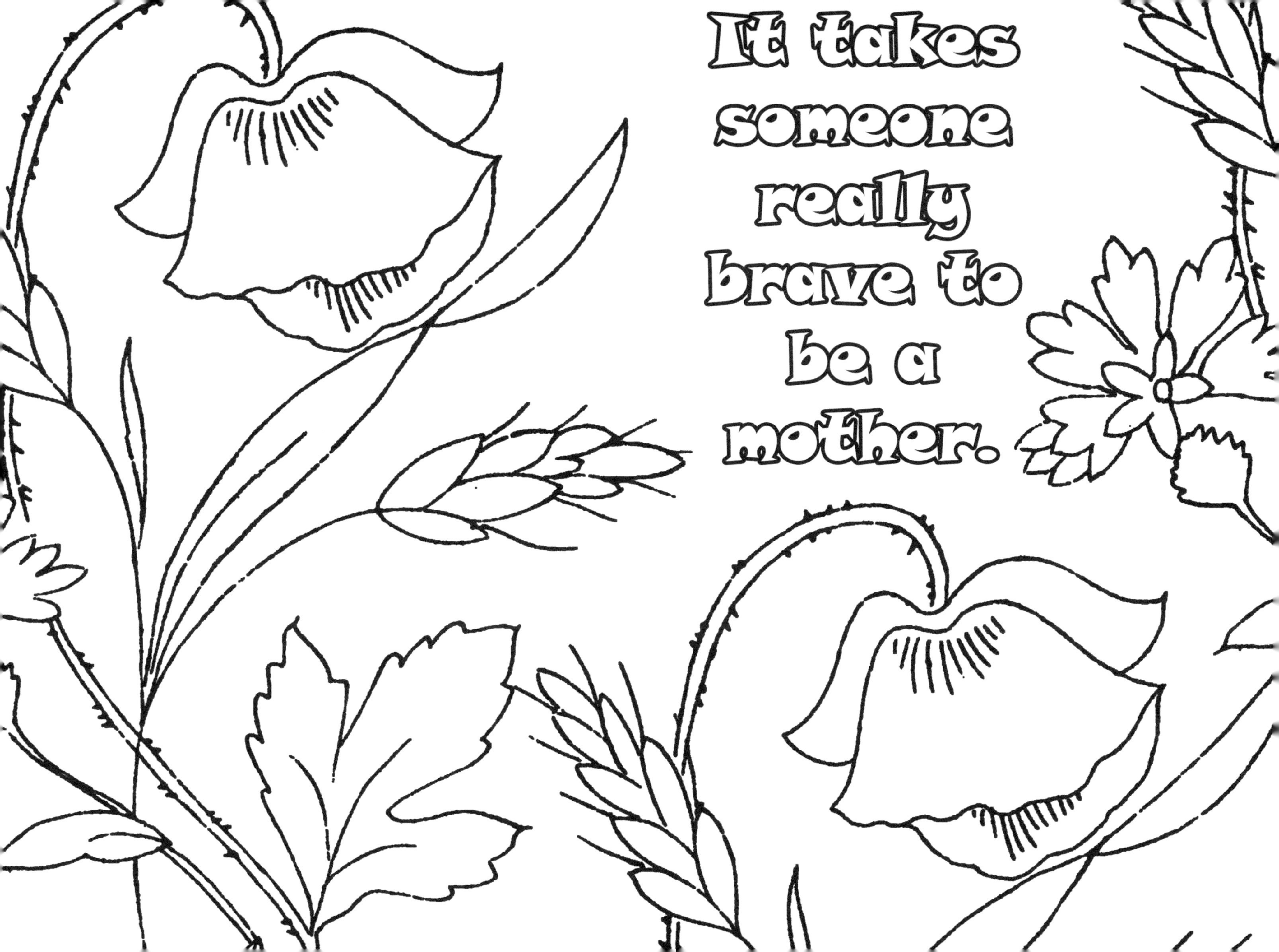
It takes
someone
really
brave to
be a
mother.

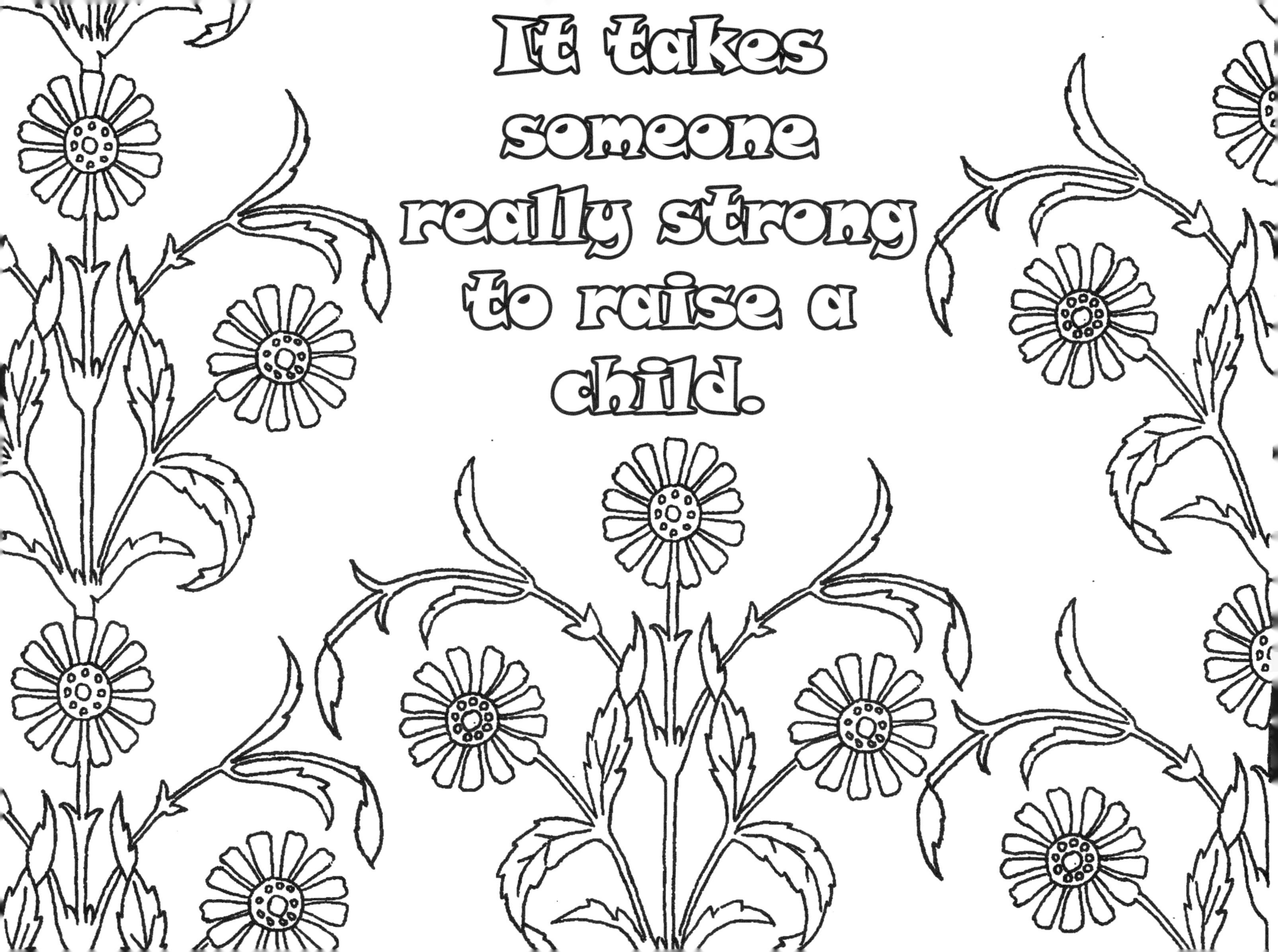
It takes someone really strong to raise a child.

It takes someone really special to love someone more than herself.

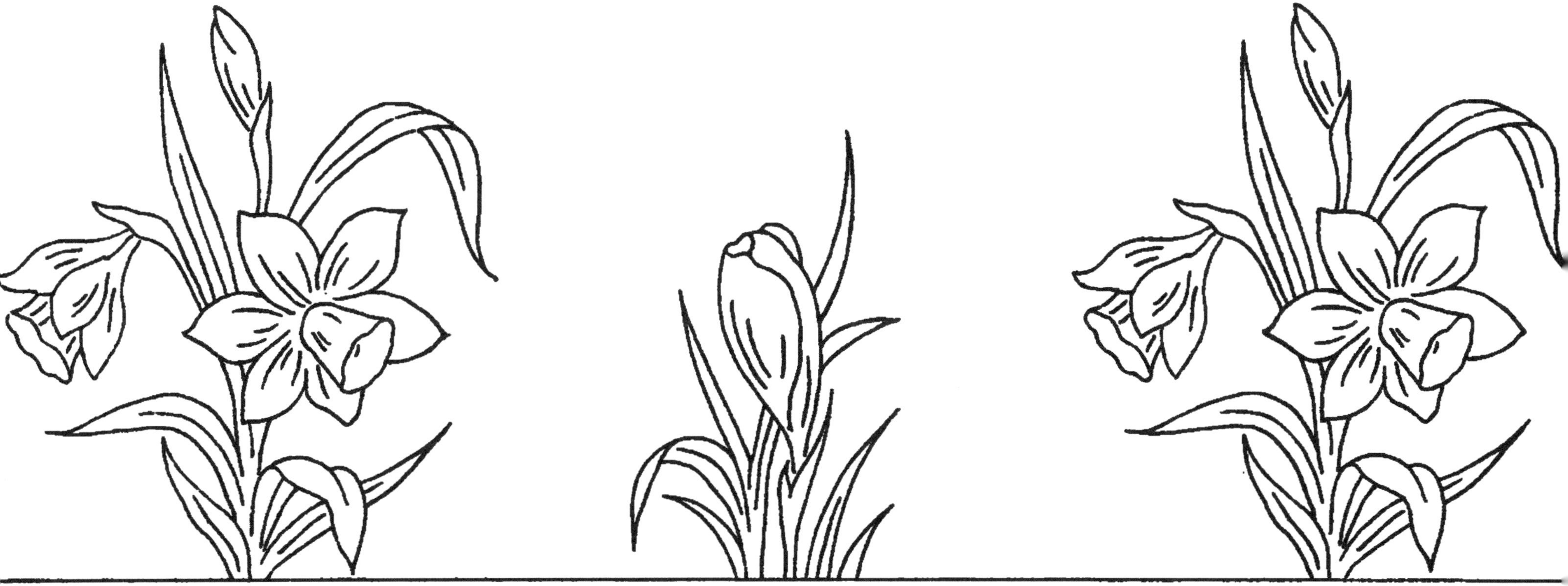

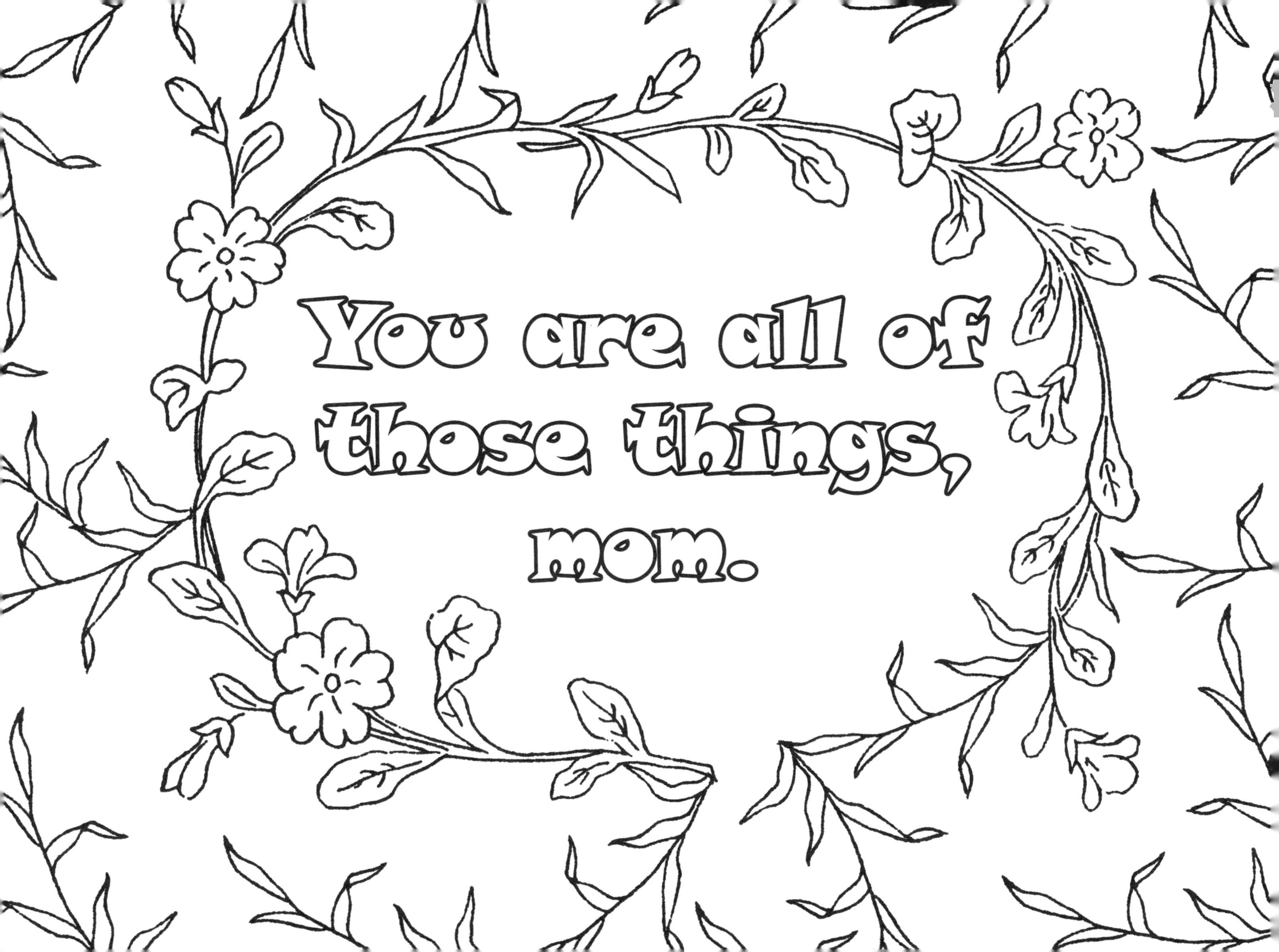
You are all of
those things,
mom.

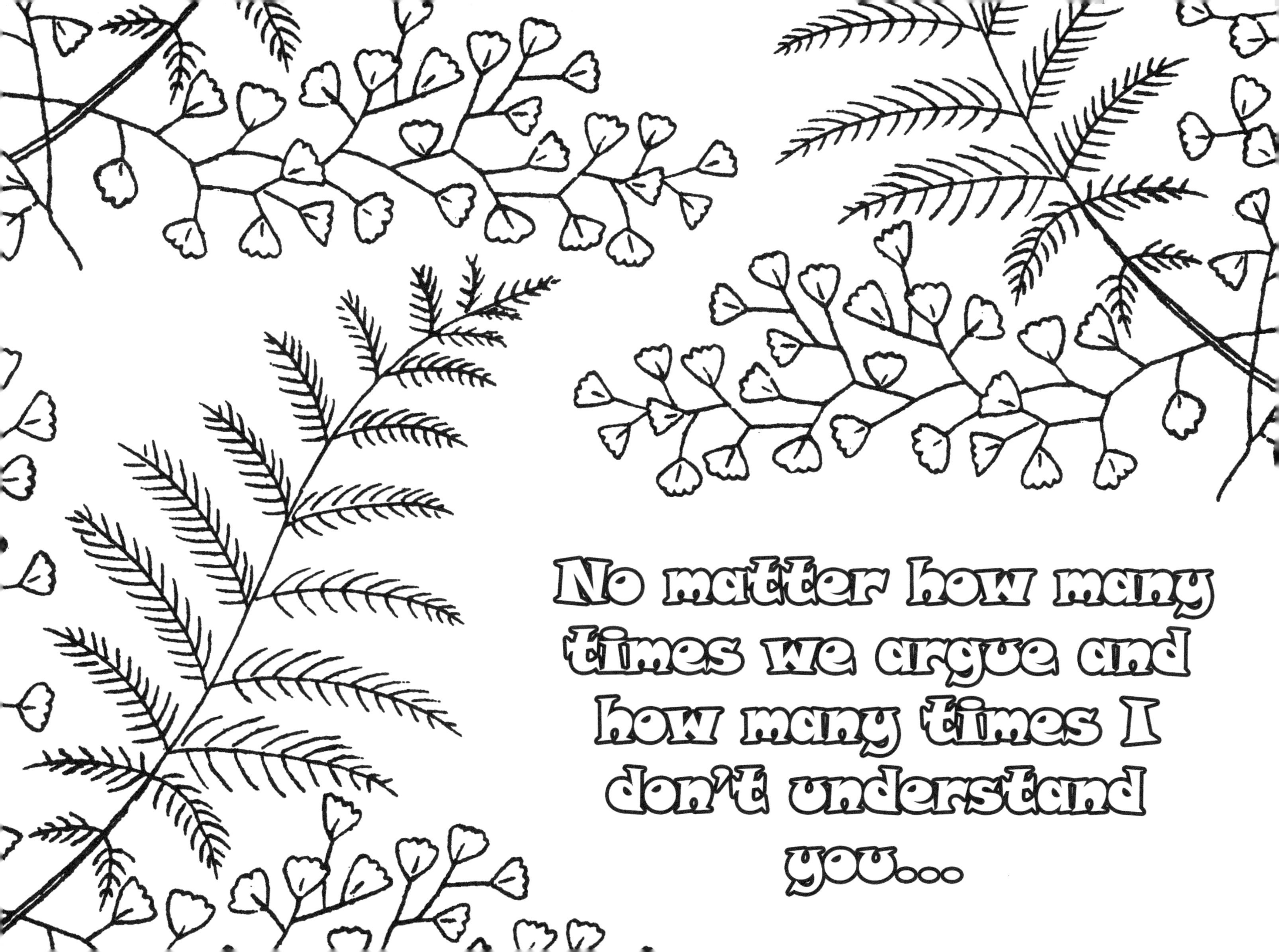

No matter how many times we argue and how many times I don't understand you...

... I still think that you are the best and will always be the greatest mom in the world.

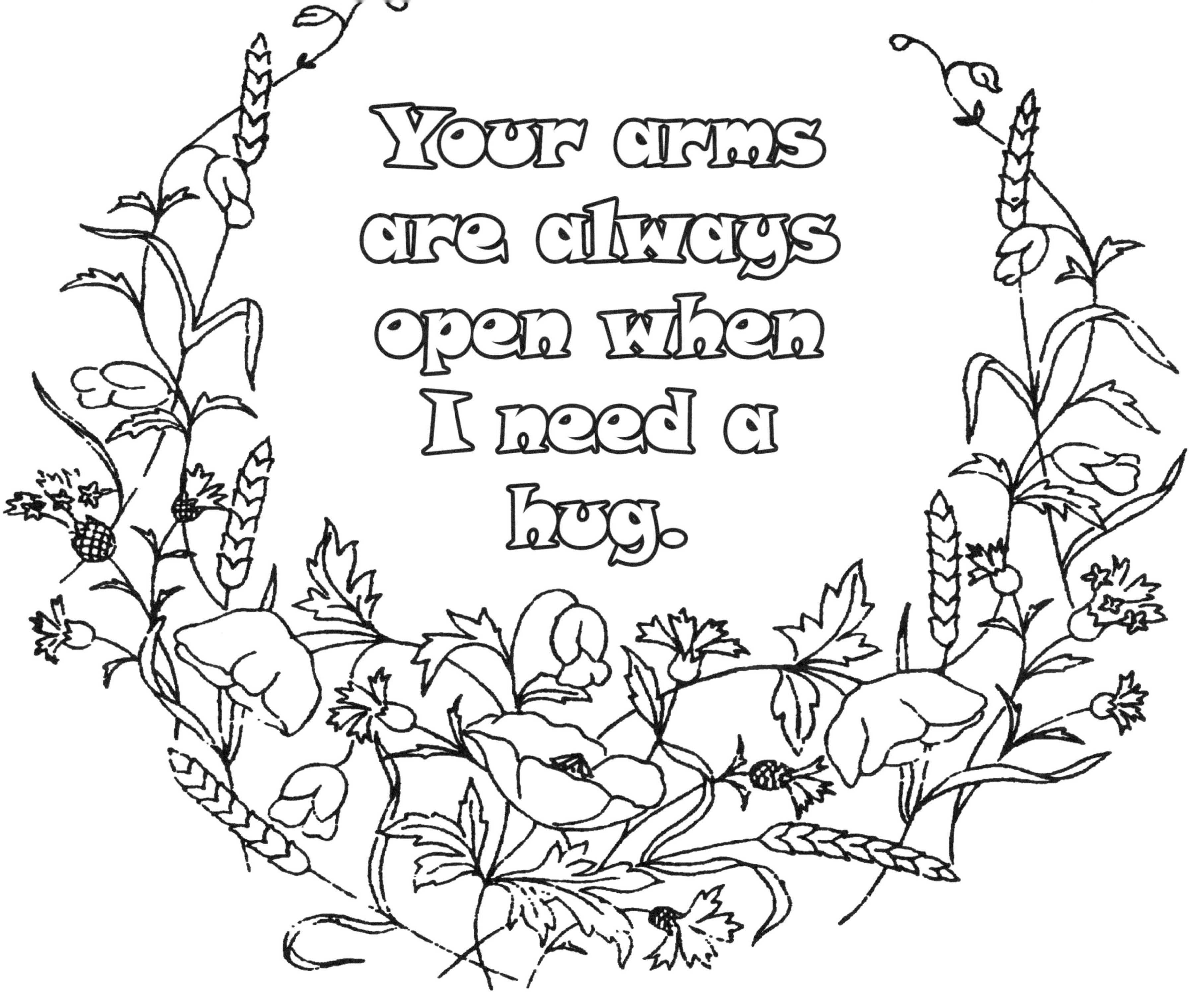
Your arms are always open when I need a hug.

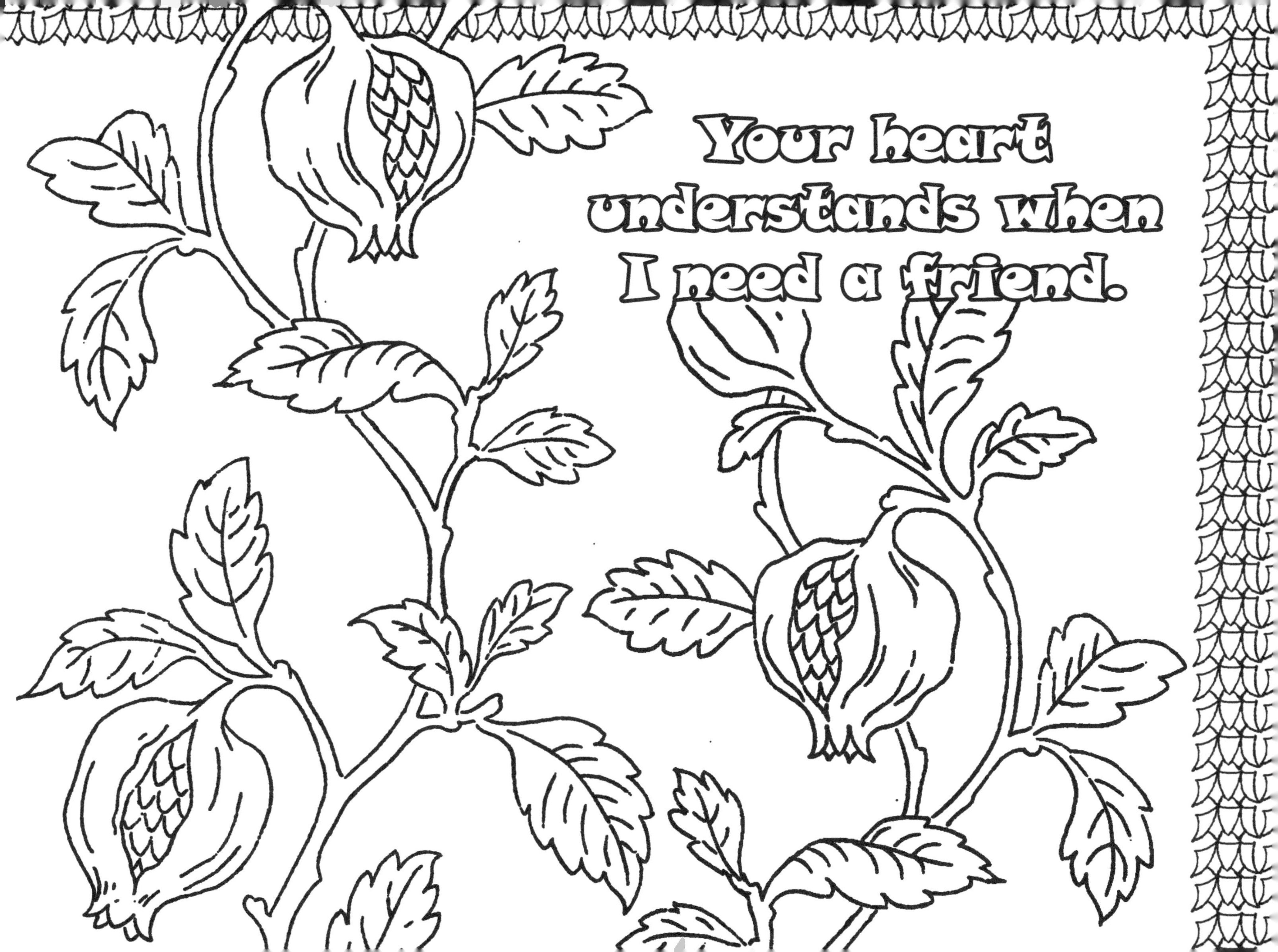
Your heart understands when I need a friend.

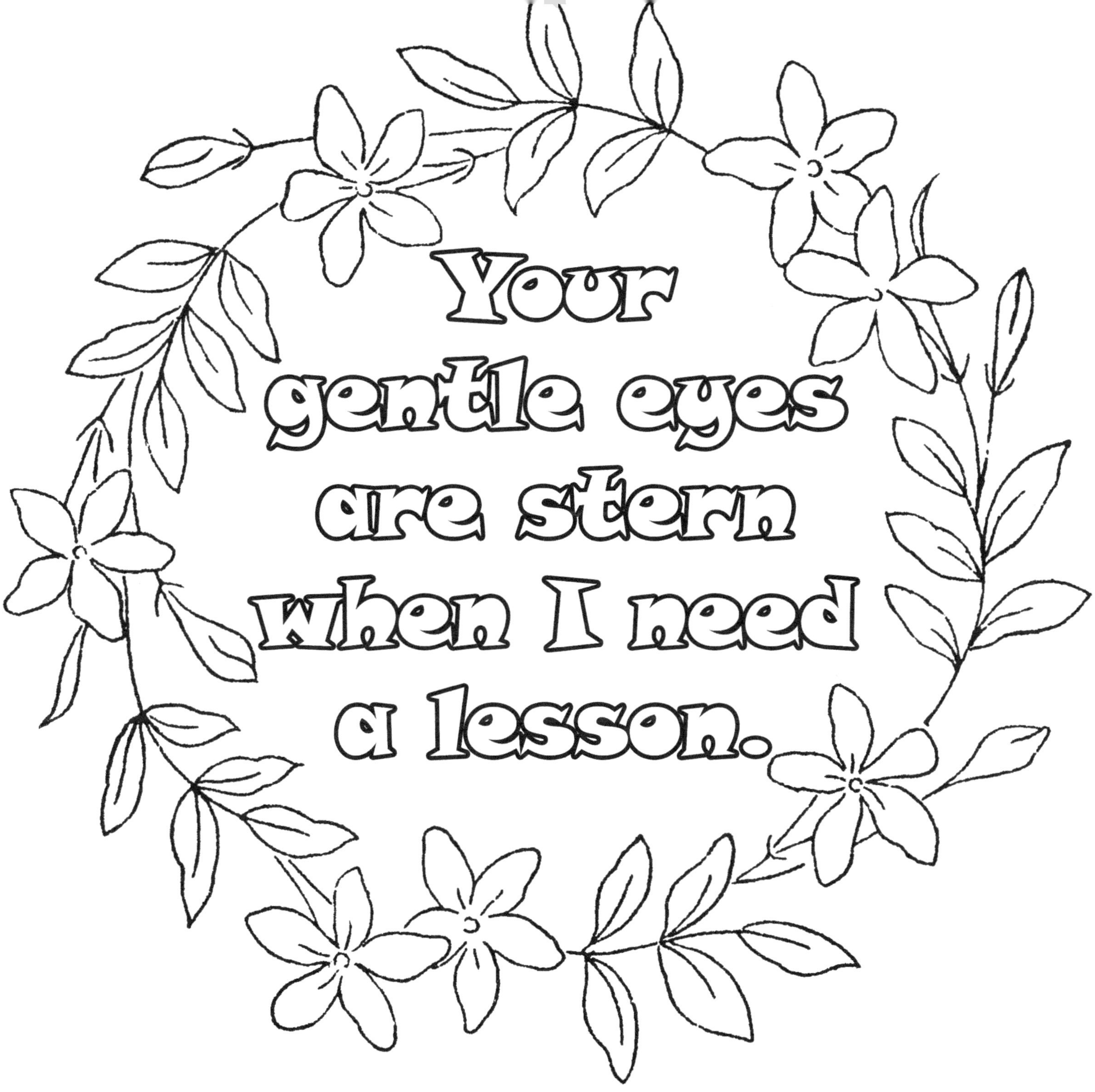
Your
gentle eyes
are stern
when I need
a lesson.

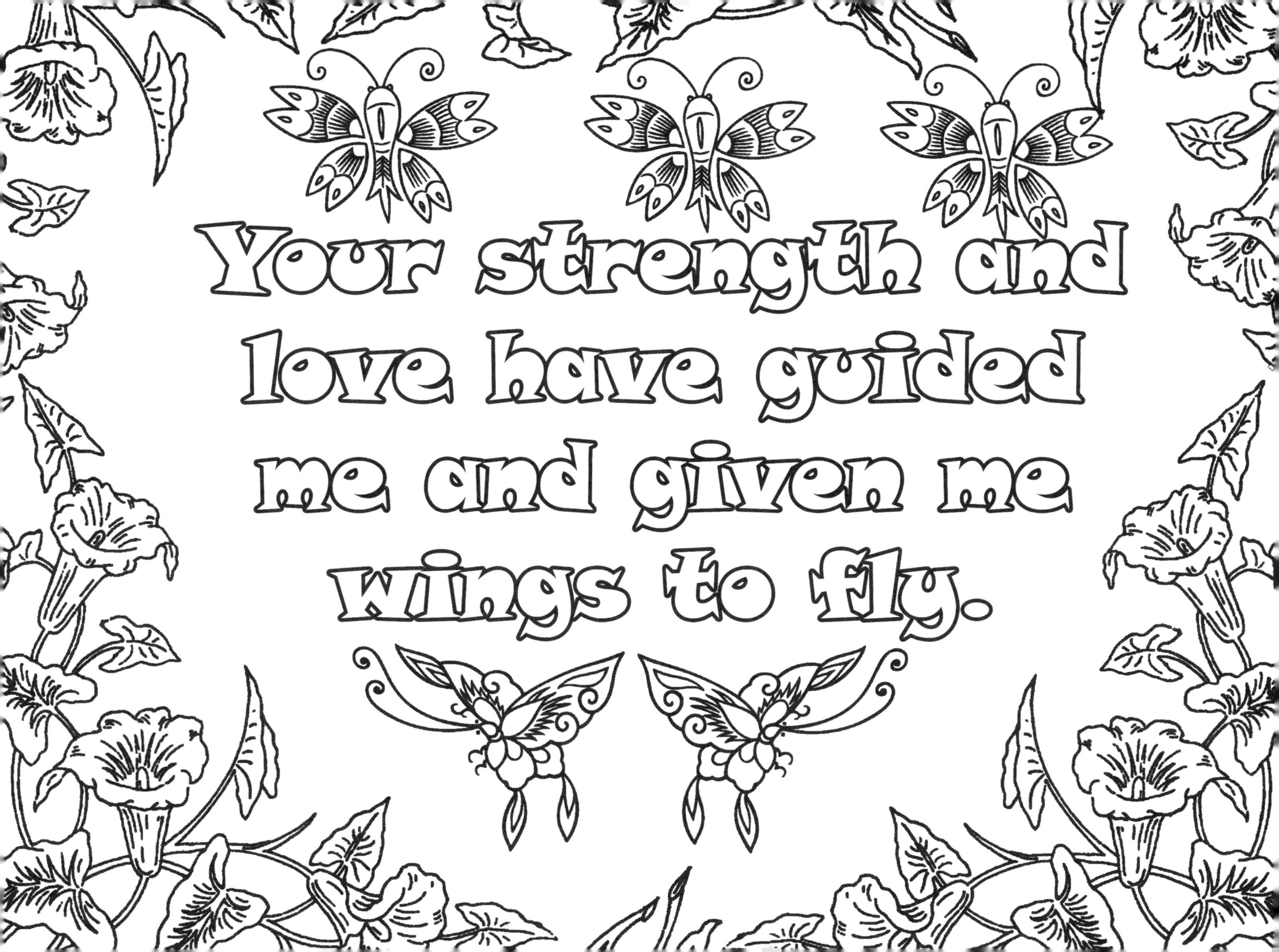
Your strength and
love have guided
me and given me
wings to fly.

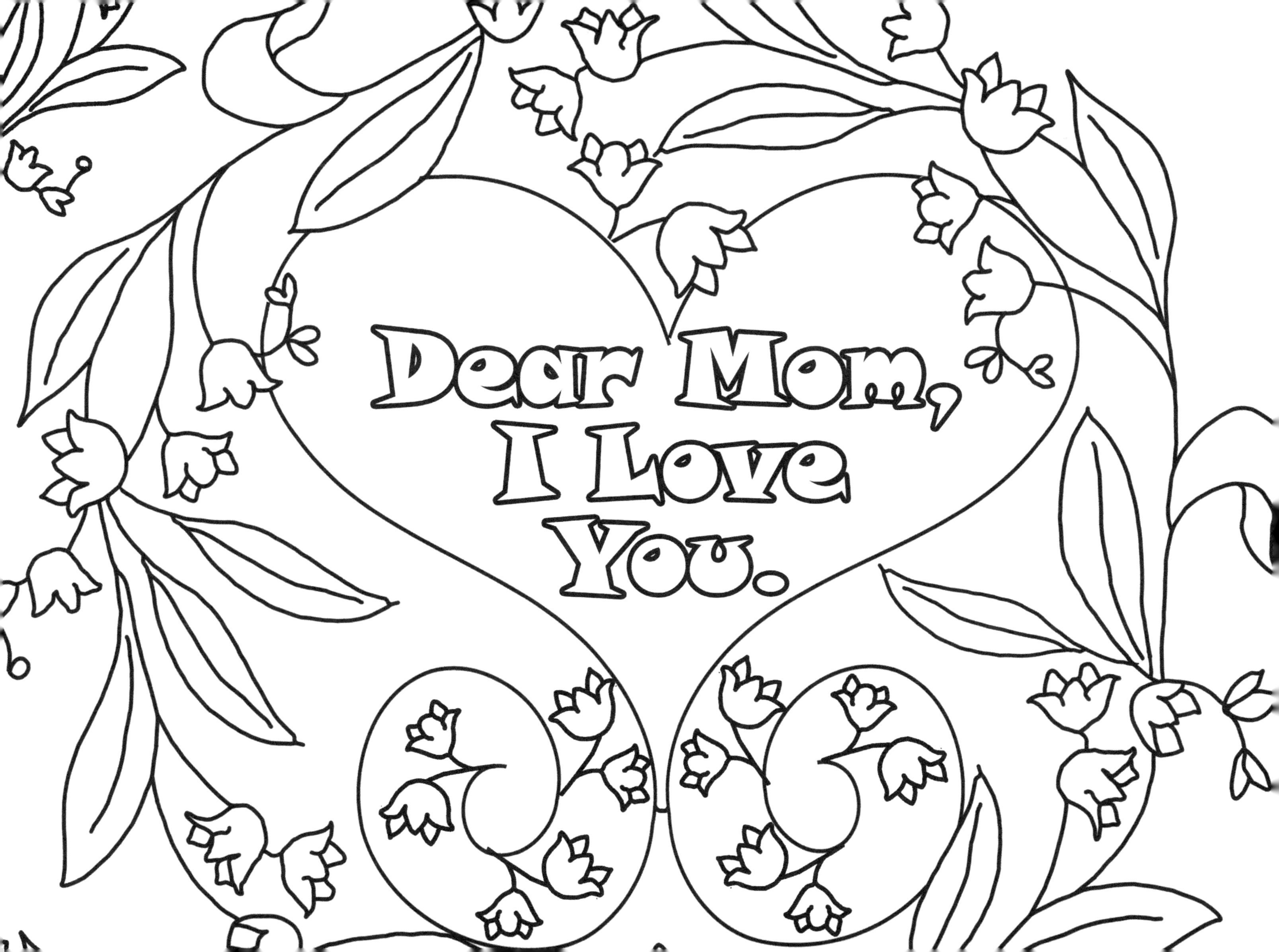
Dear Mom,
I Love
You.

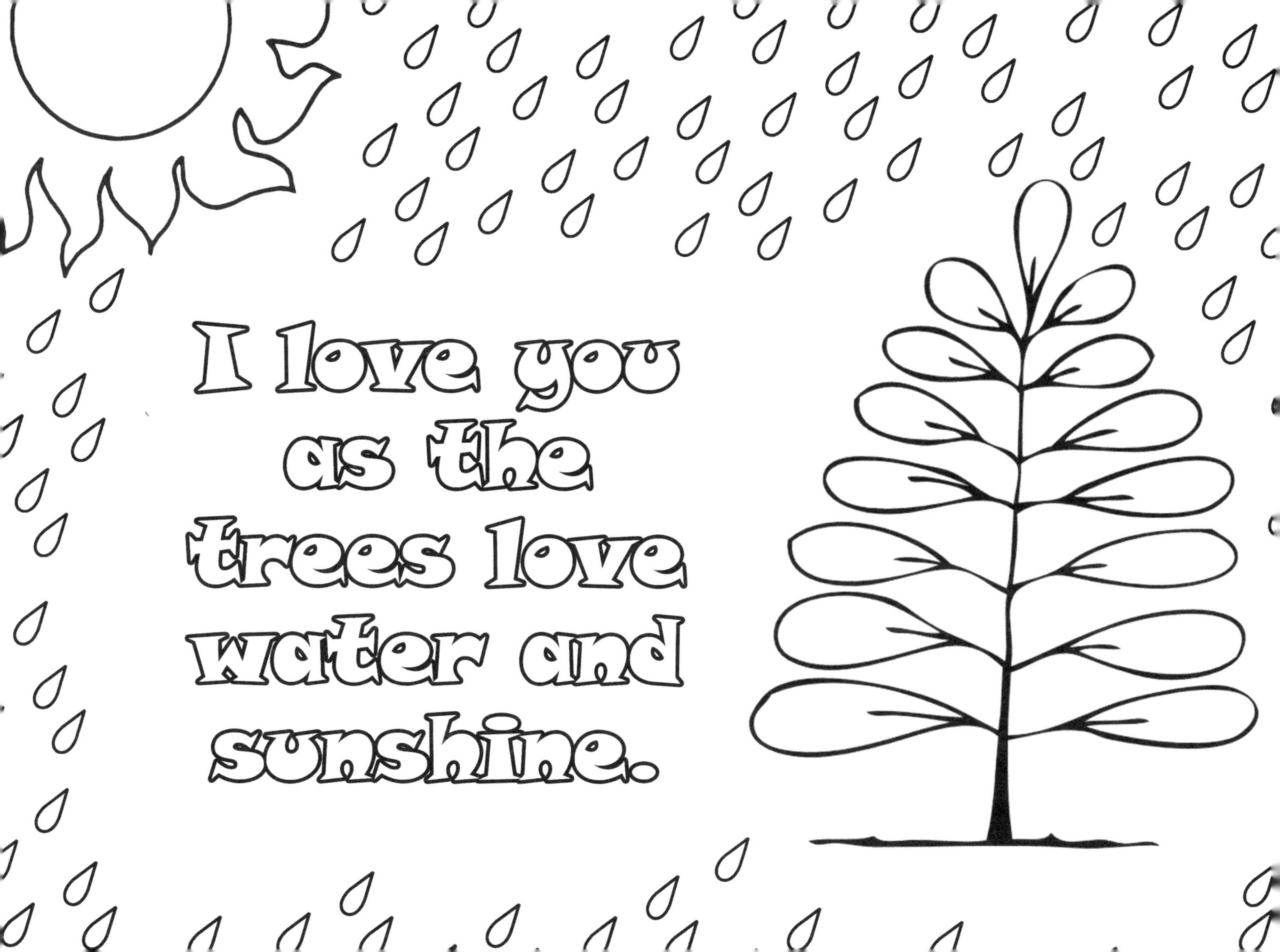
I love you
as the
trees love
water and
sunshine.

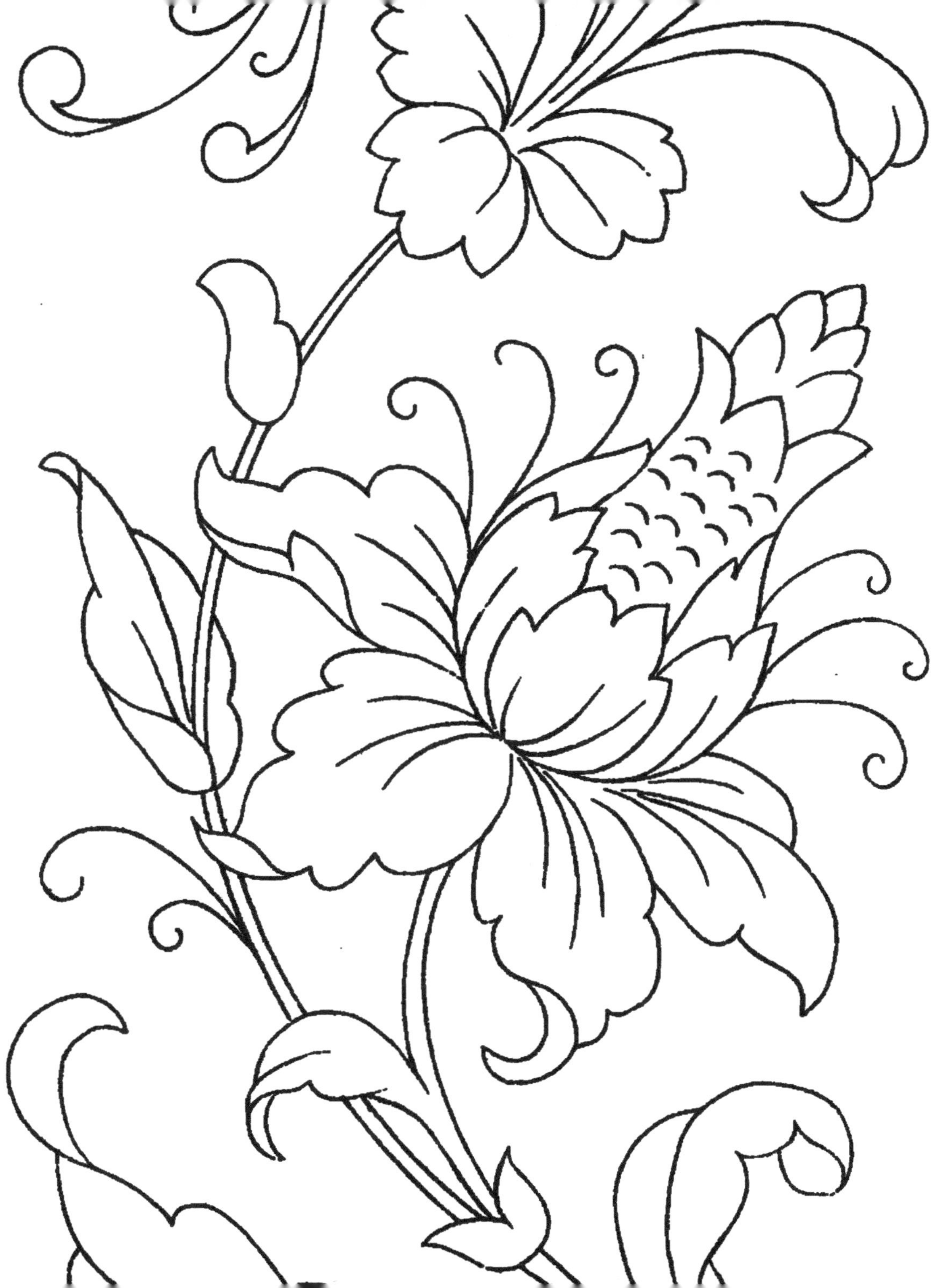

You help me grow, prosper, and reach great heights.

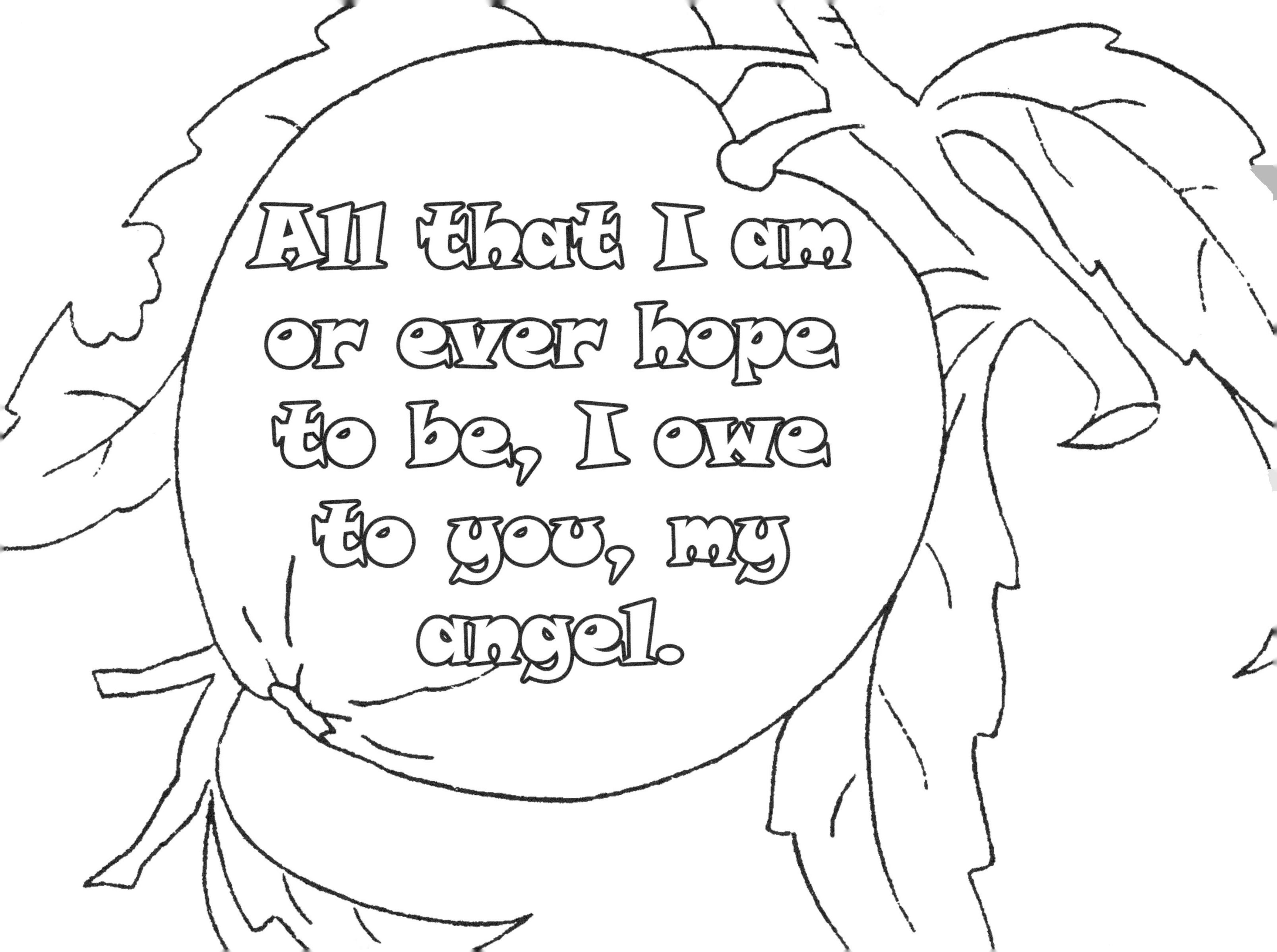
All that I am
or ever hope
to be, I owe
to you, my
angel.

The more I grow, the more I realize ...

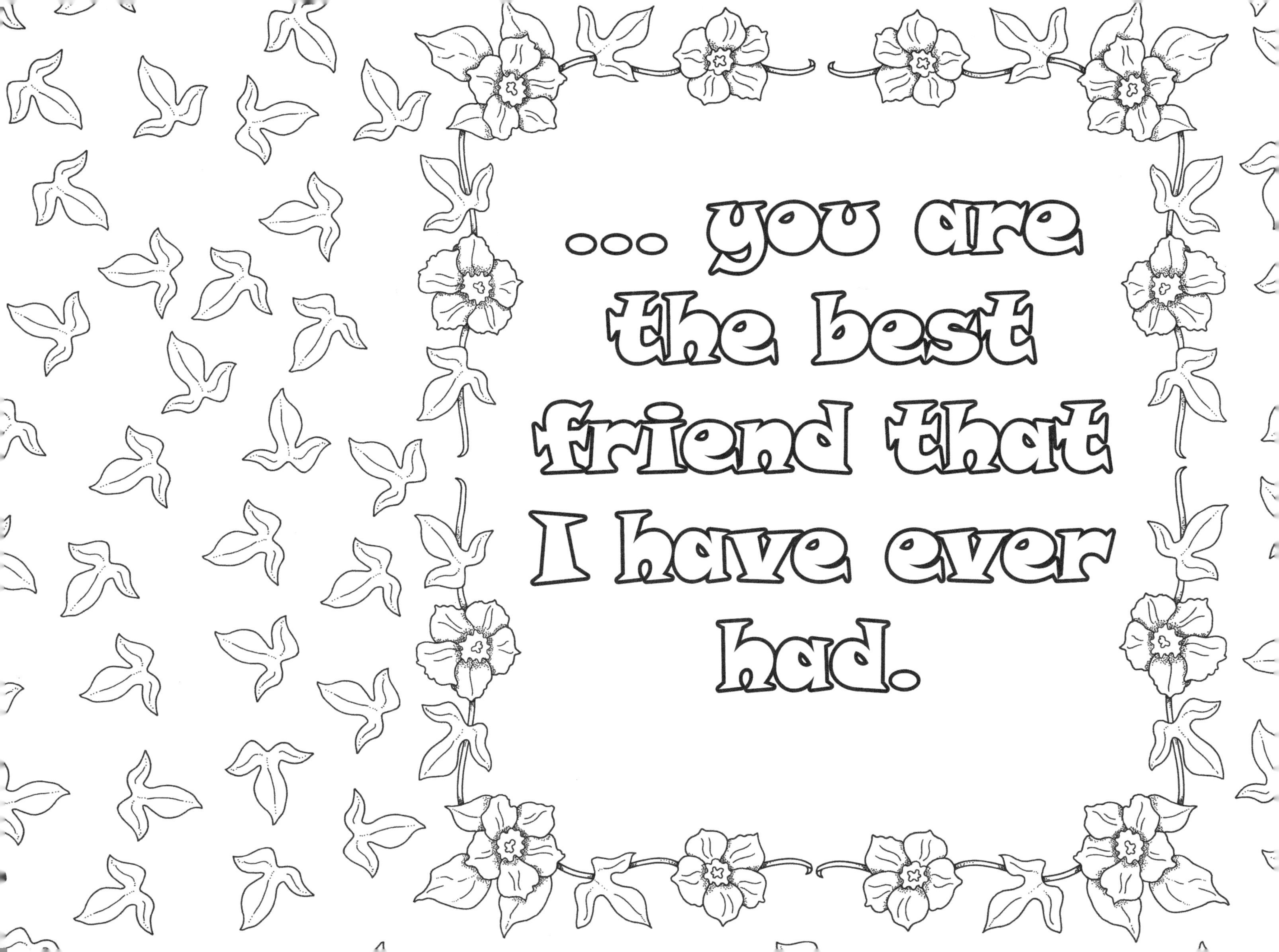
... you are
the best
friend that
I have ever
had.

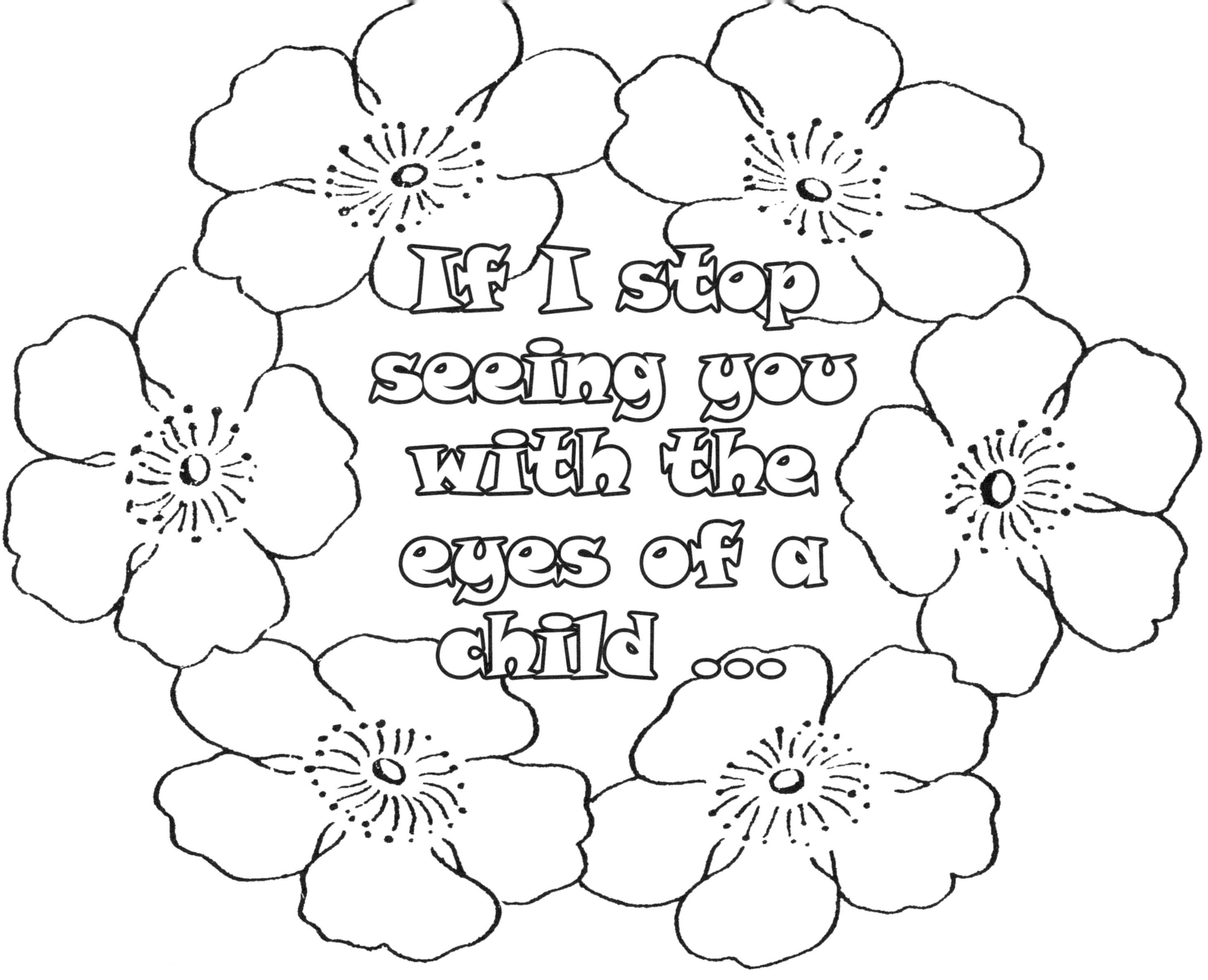
If I stop
seeing you
with the
eyes of a
child ...

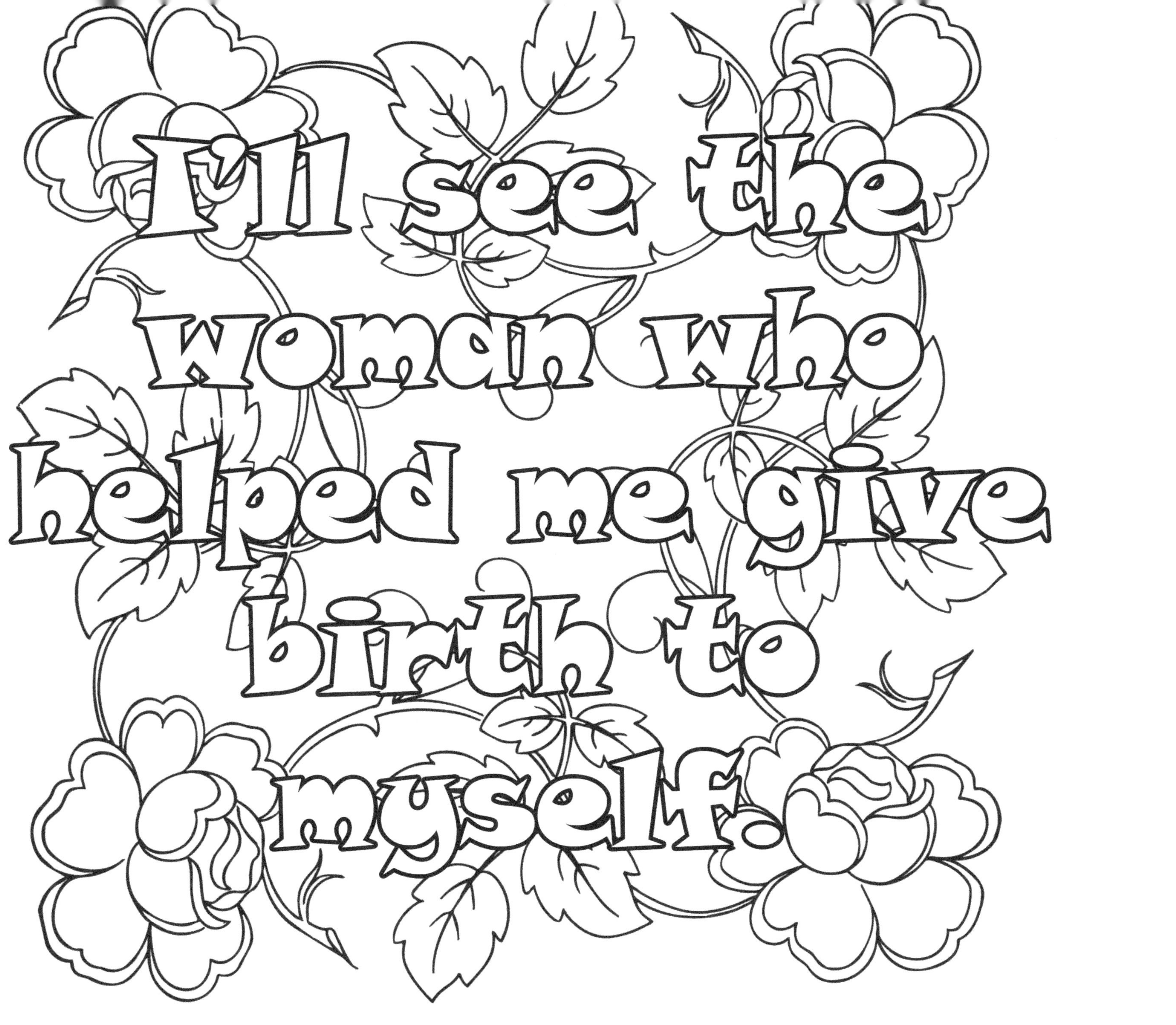
I'll see the woman who helped me give birth to myself.

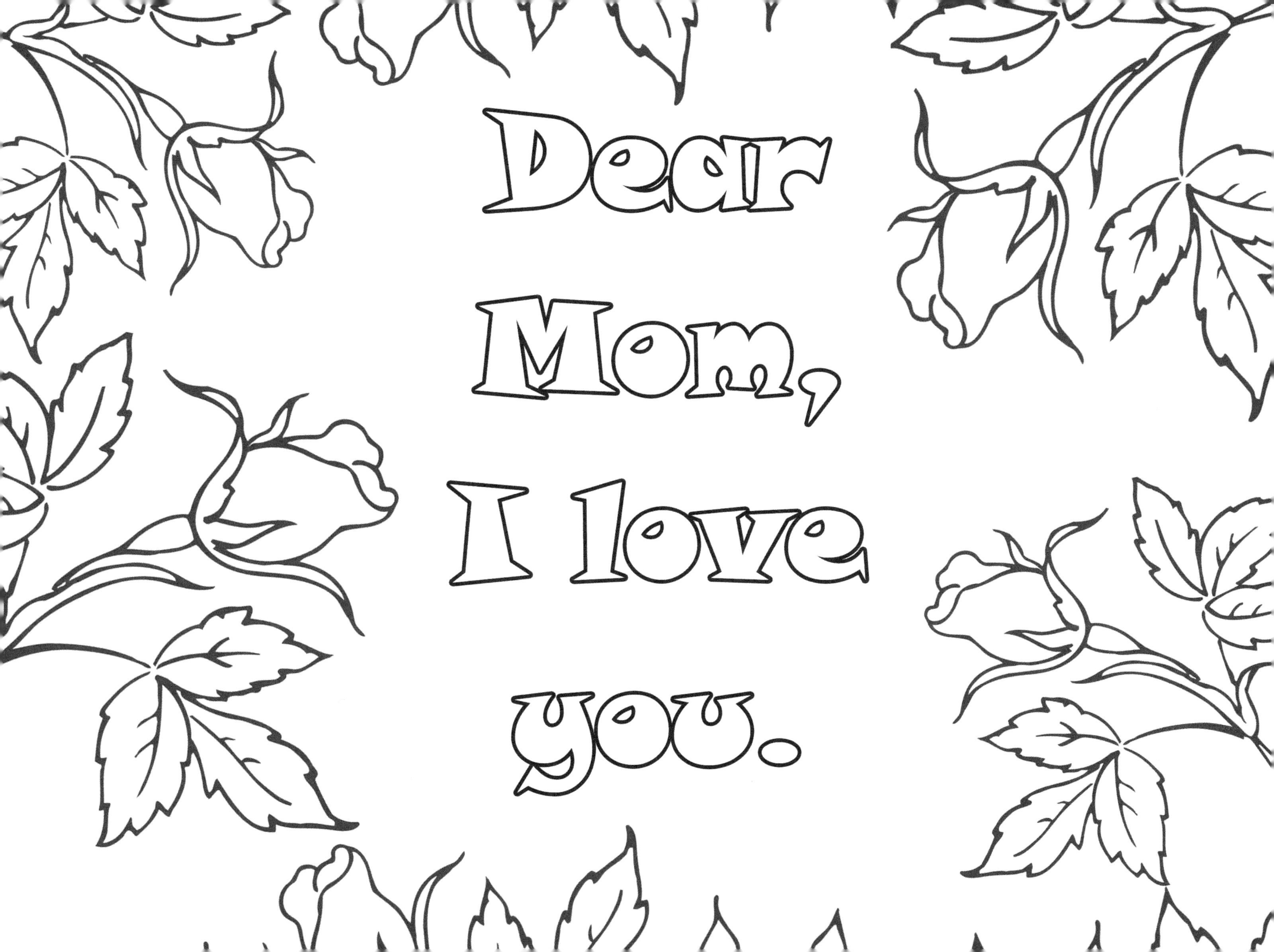
Dear
Mom,
I love
you.

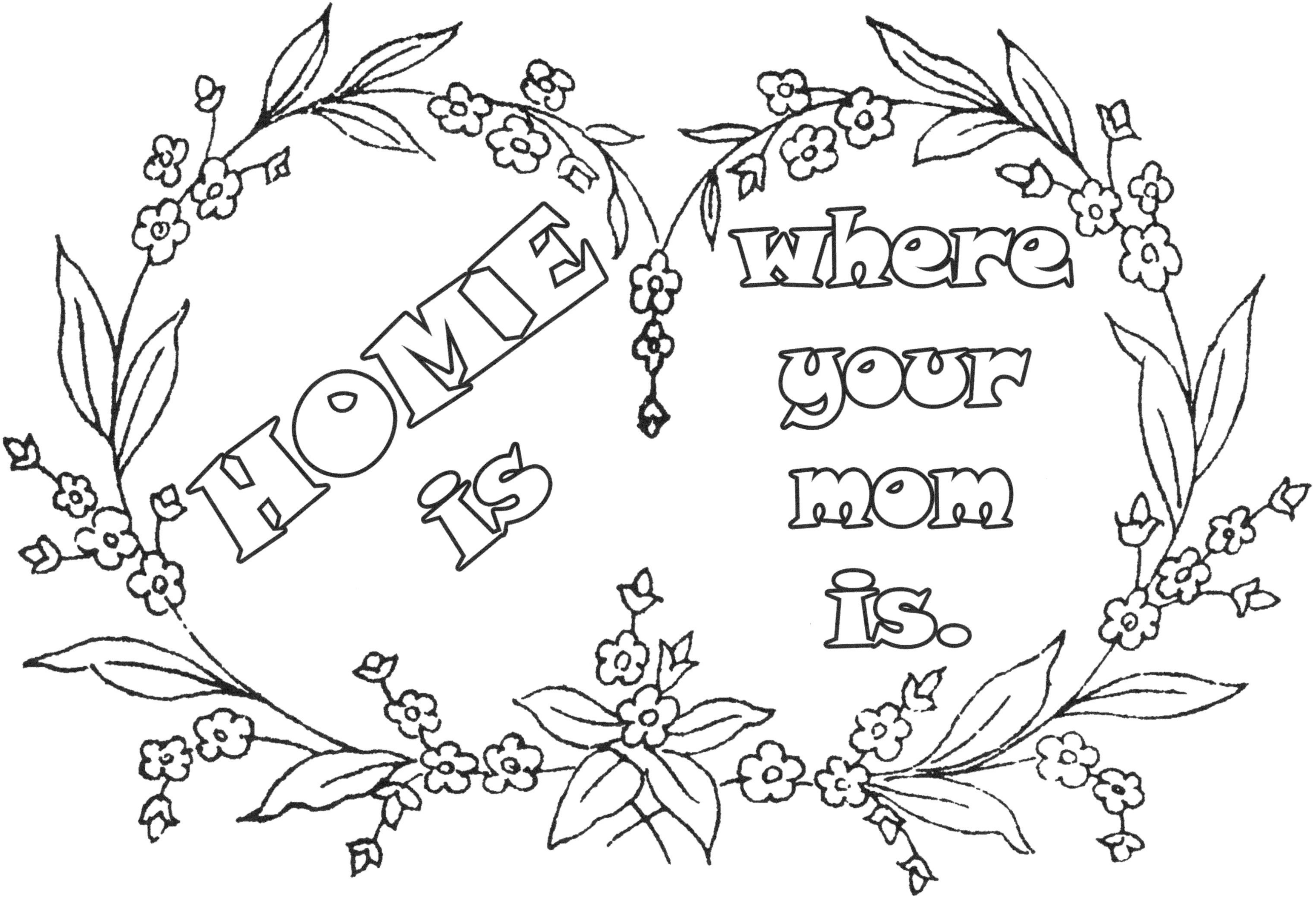
HOME is
where your mom is.

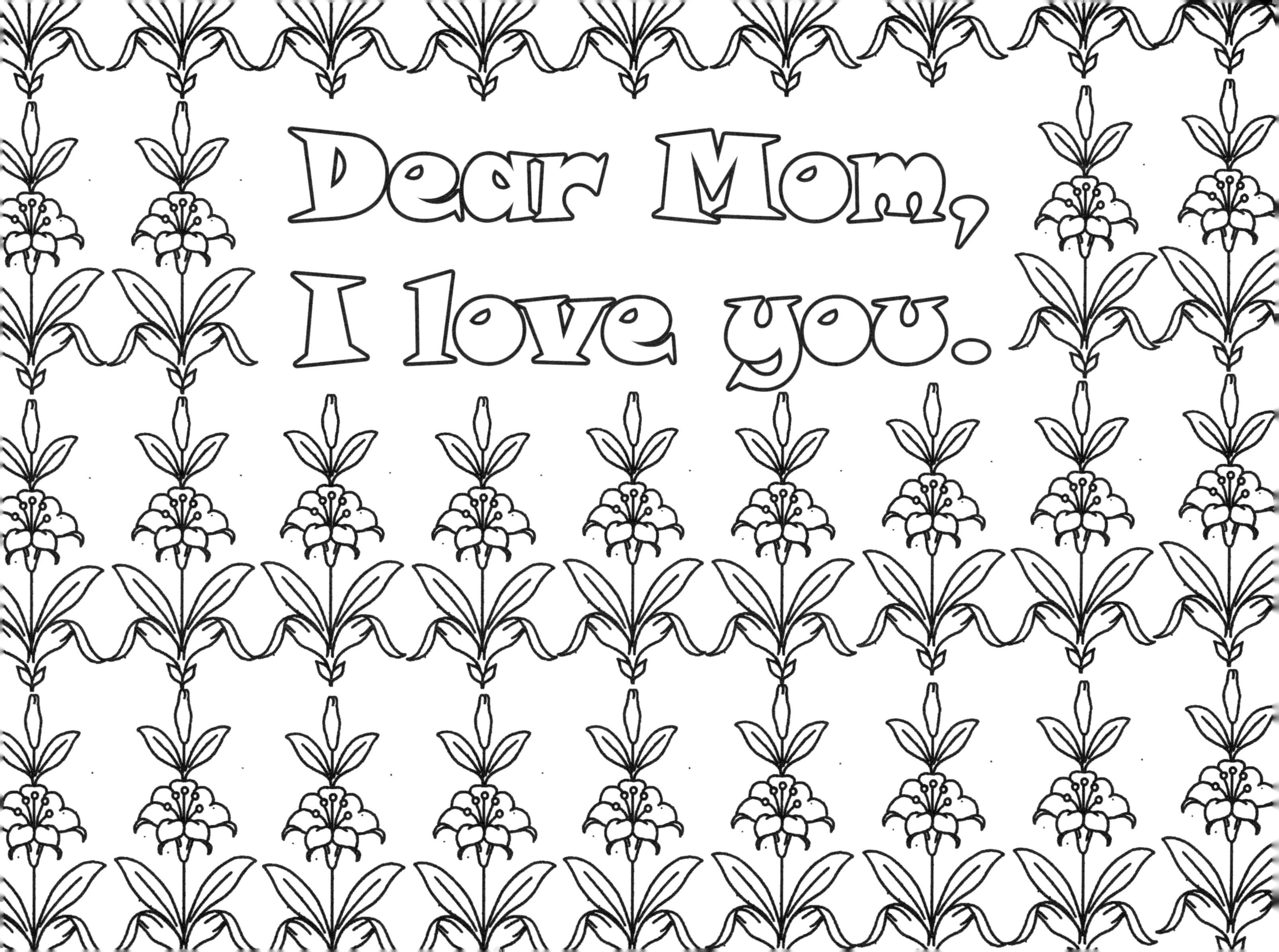
Dear Mom,
I love you.

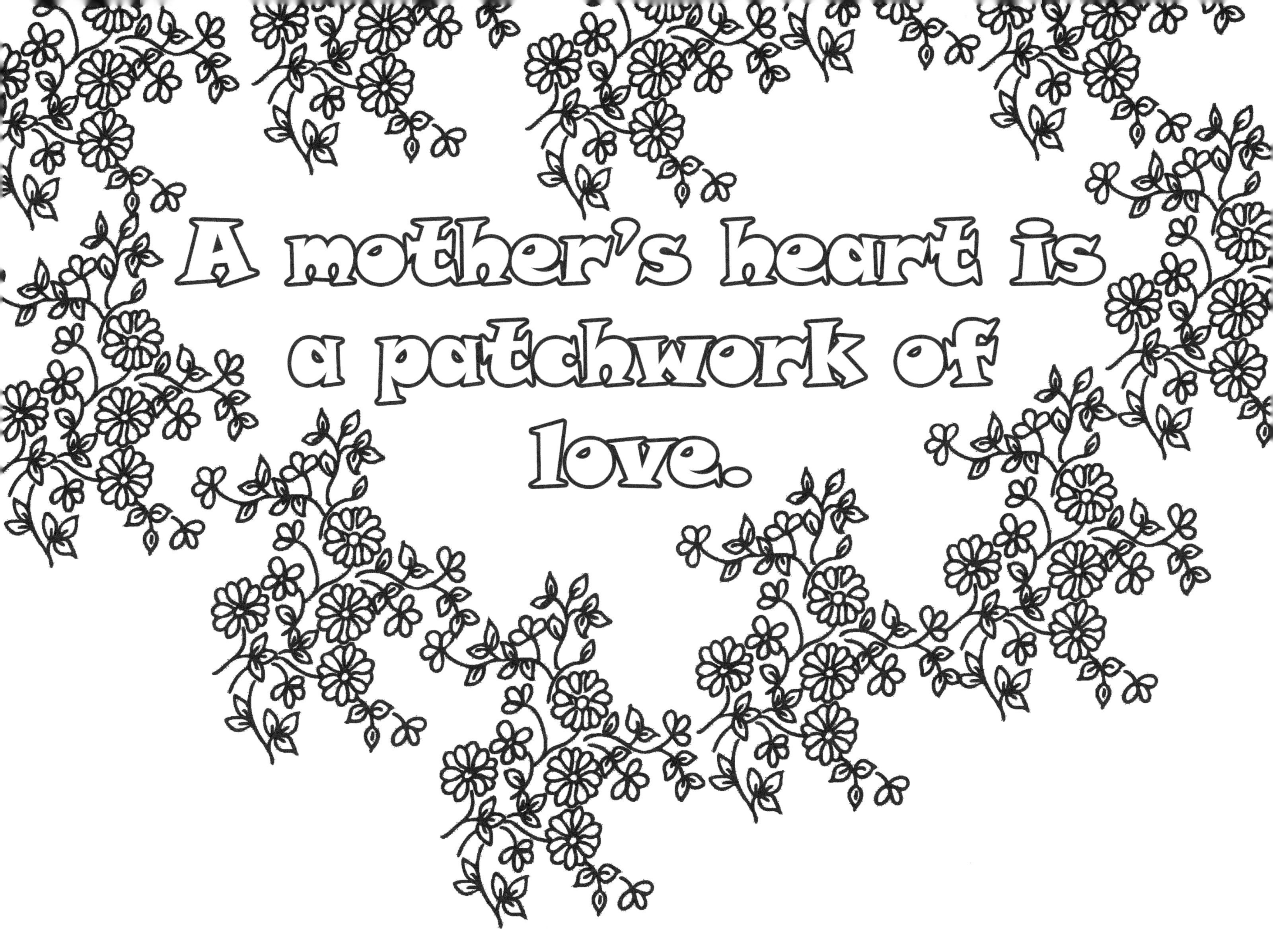
A mother's heart is
a patchwork of
love.

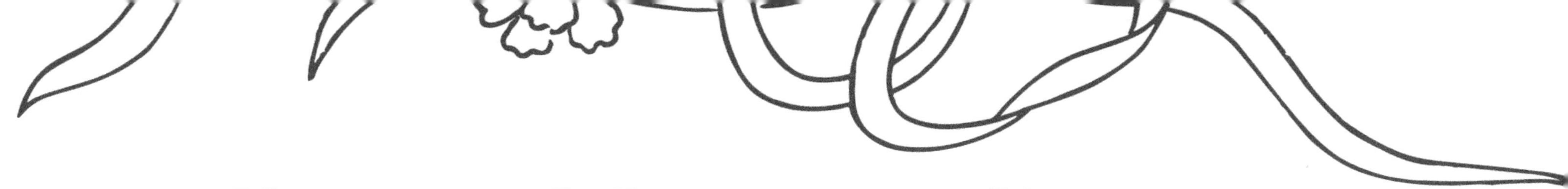

The ribbons of your love are woven around my heart.

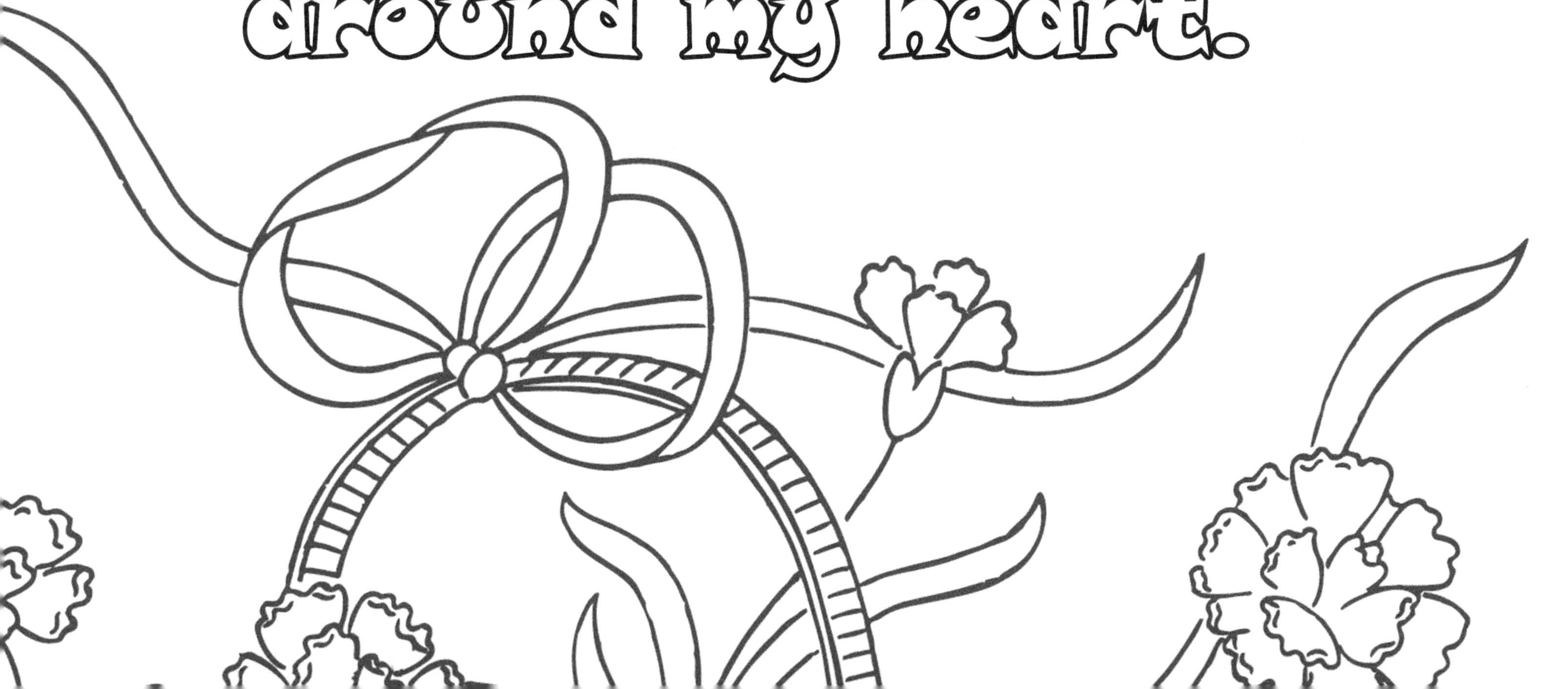

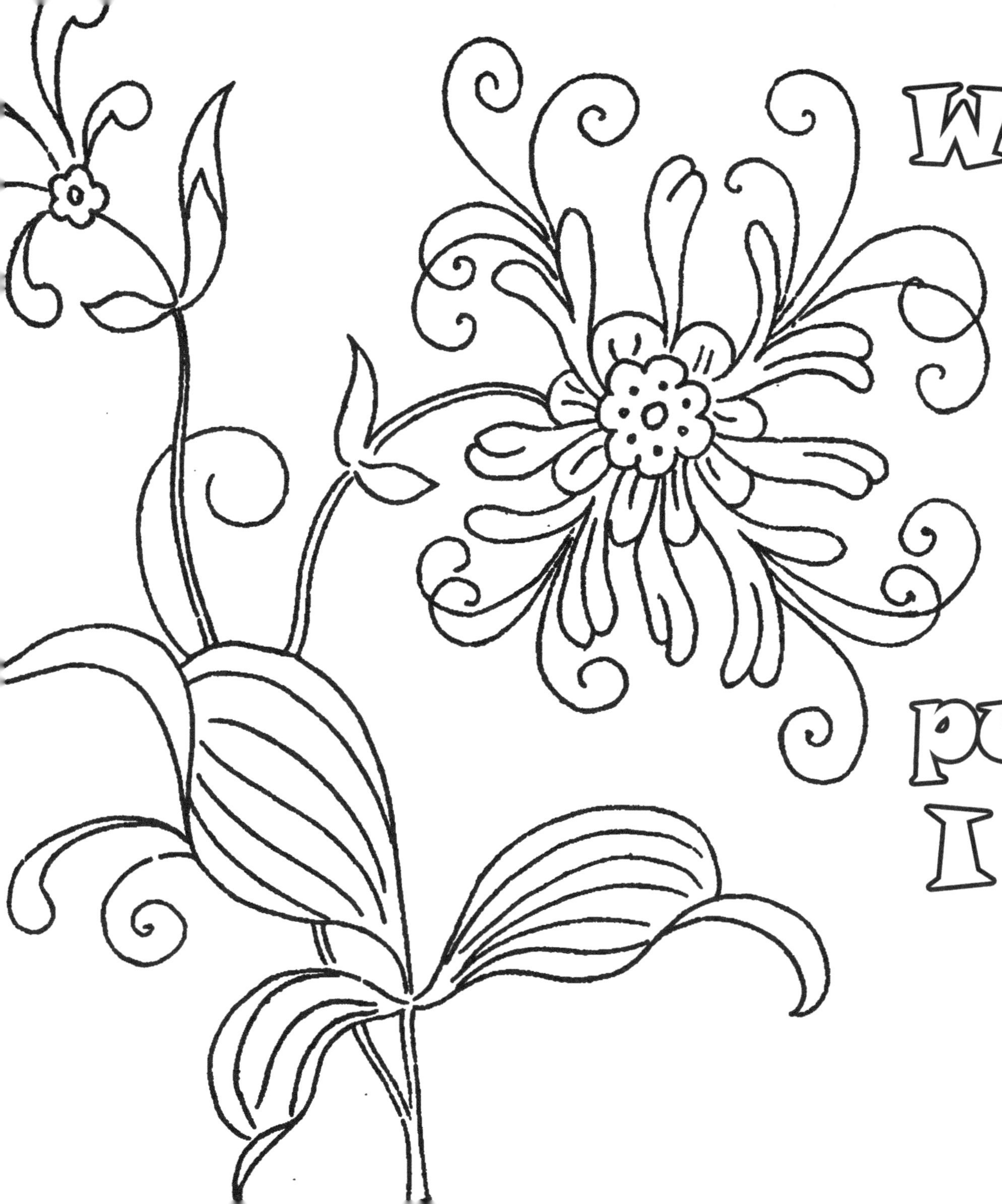

When I look
at you,
I am
looking
at the
purest love
I will ever
know.

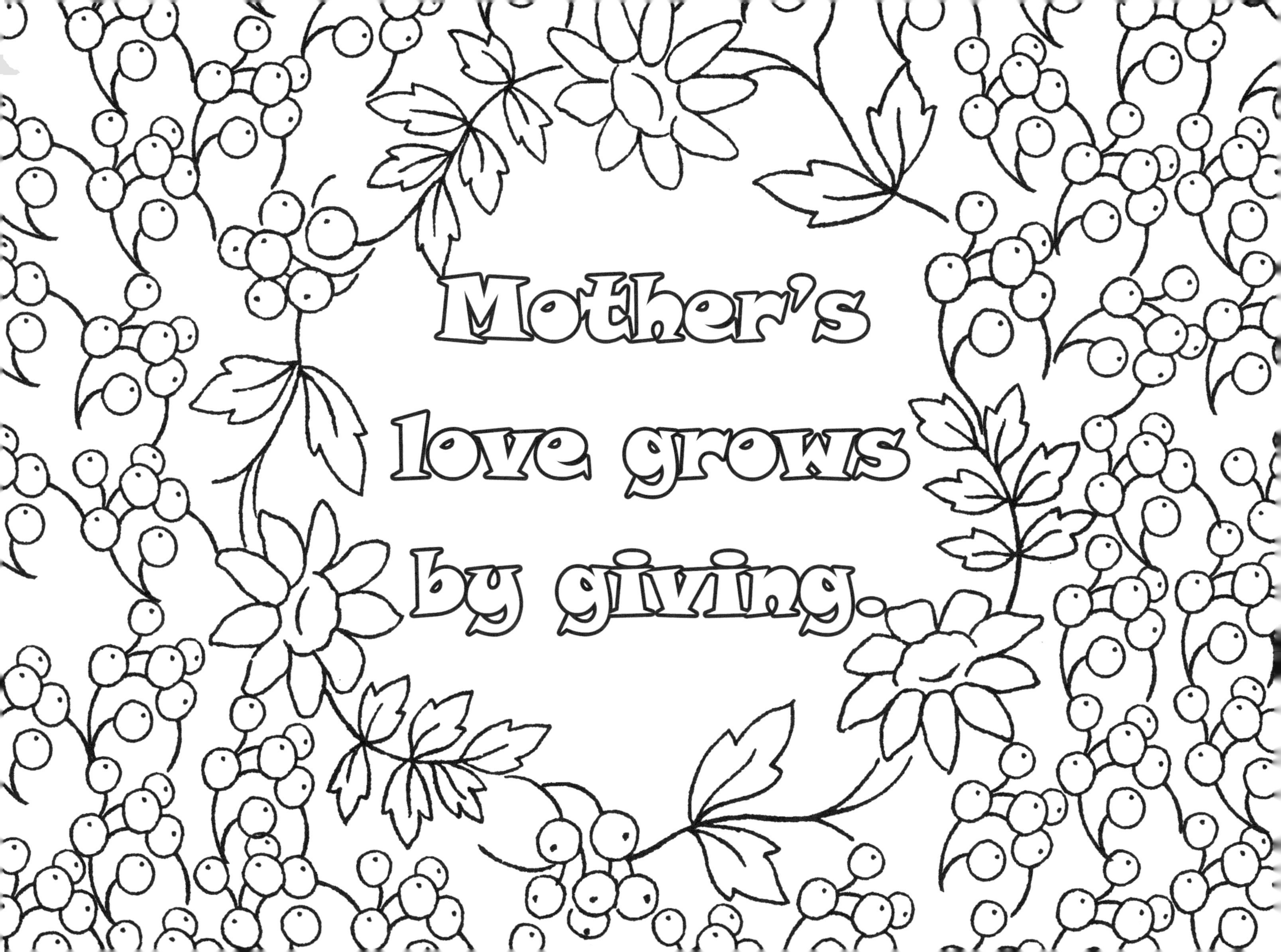
Mother's love grows by giving.

You love me

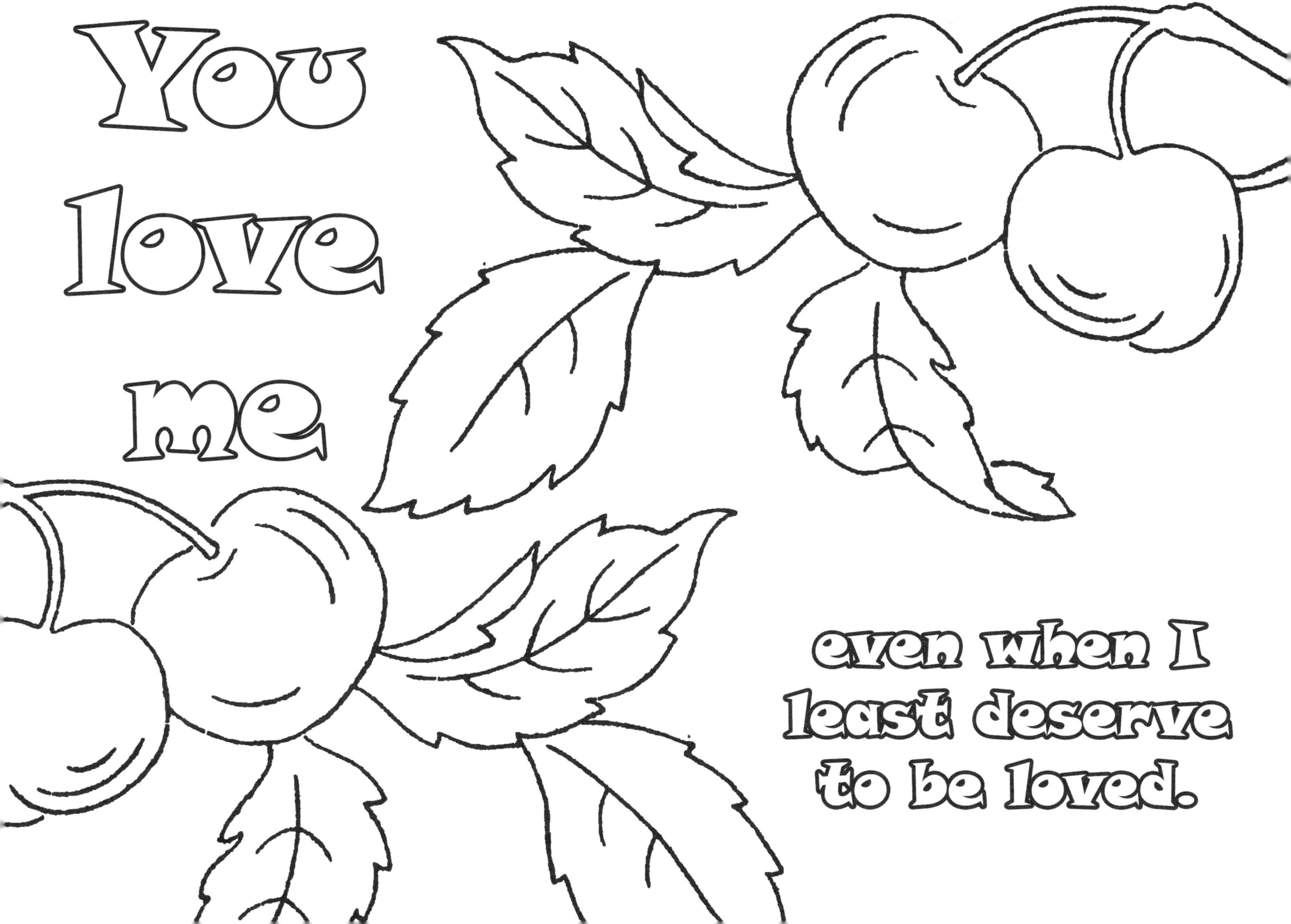

even when I least deserve to be loved.

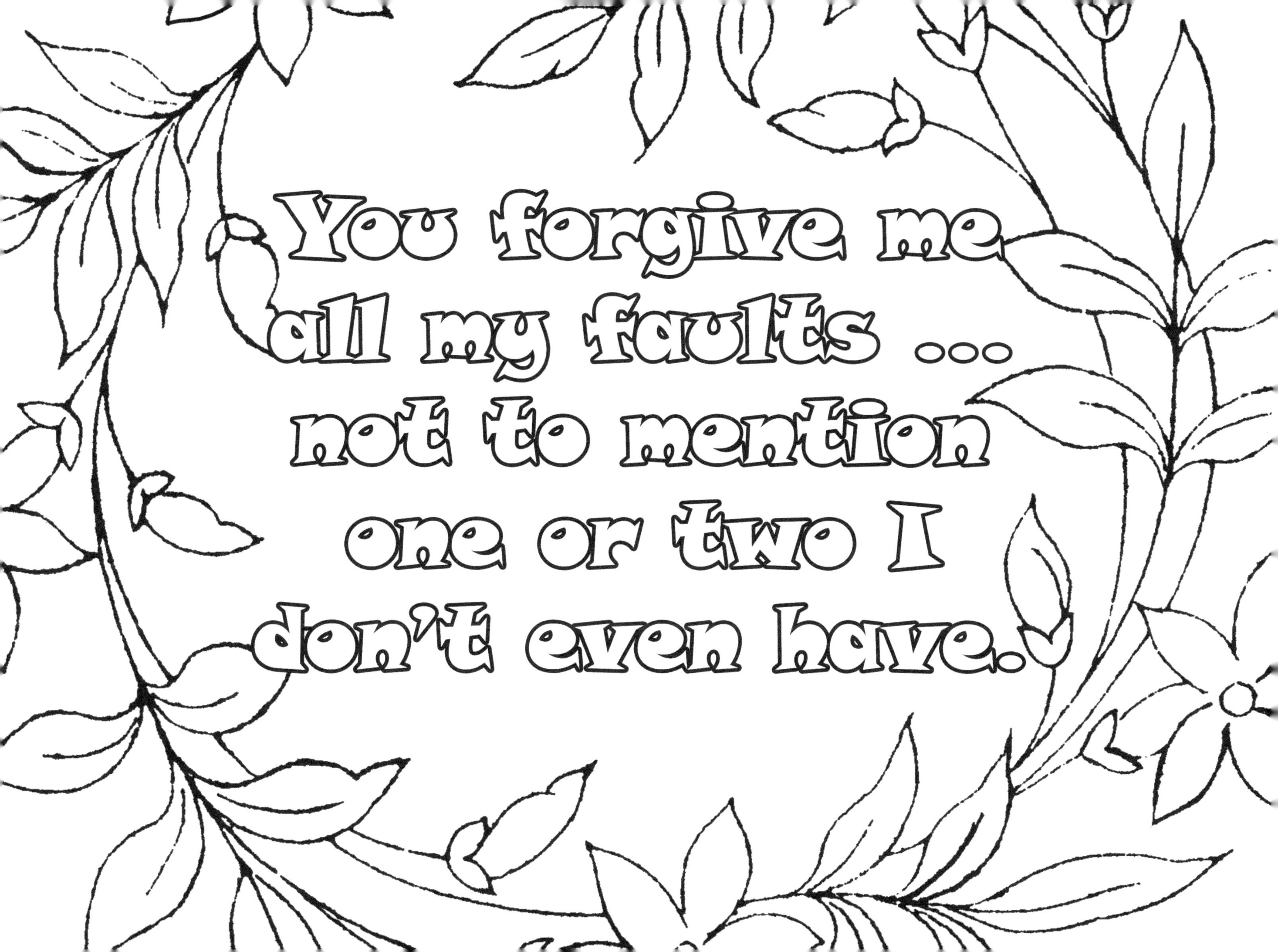
You forgive me
all my faults ...
not to mention
one or two I
don't even have.

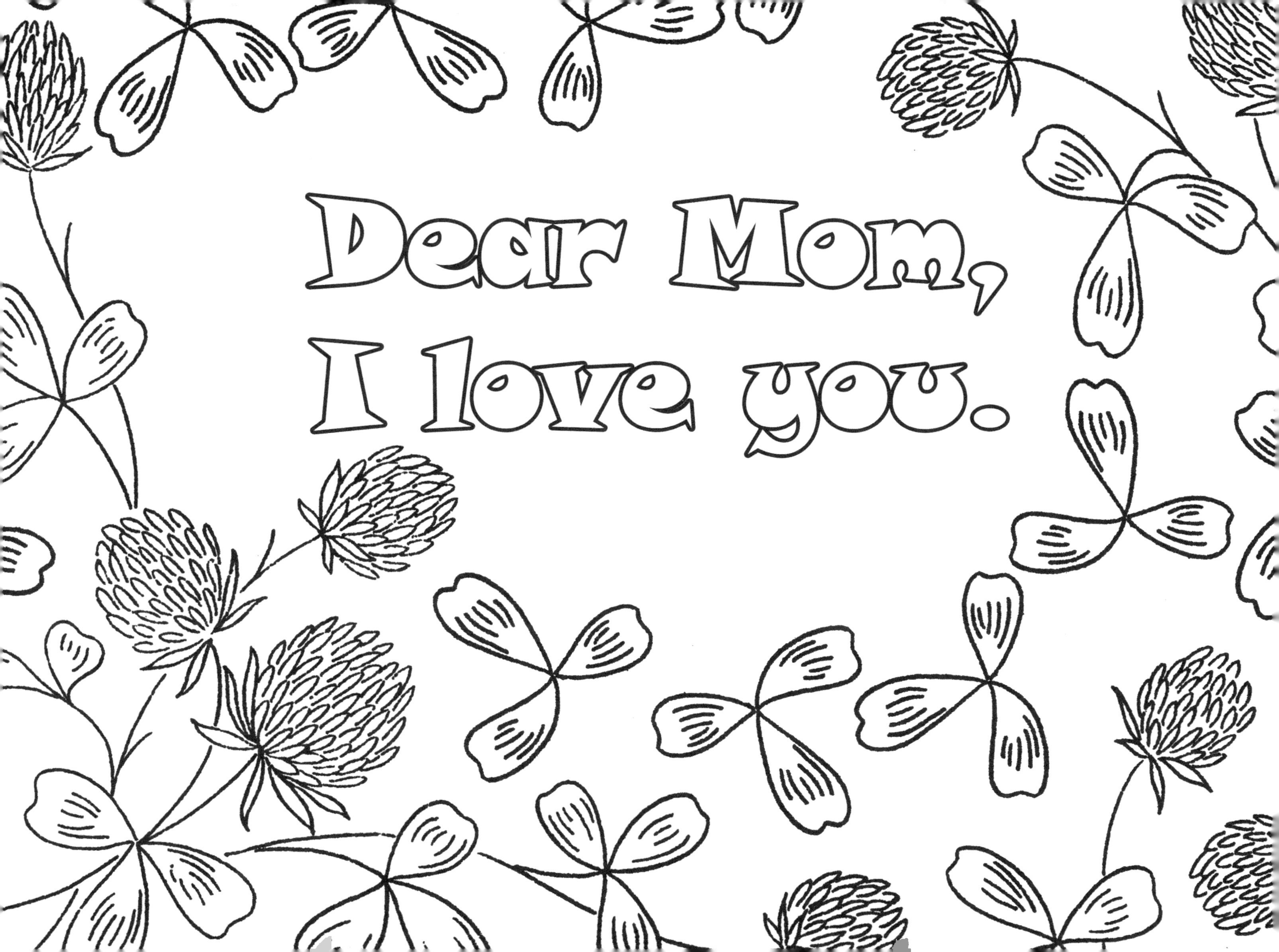
Dear Mom,
I love you.

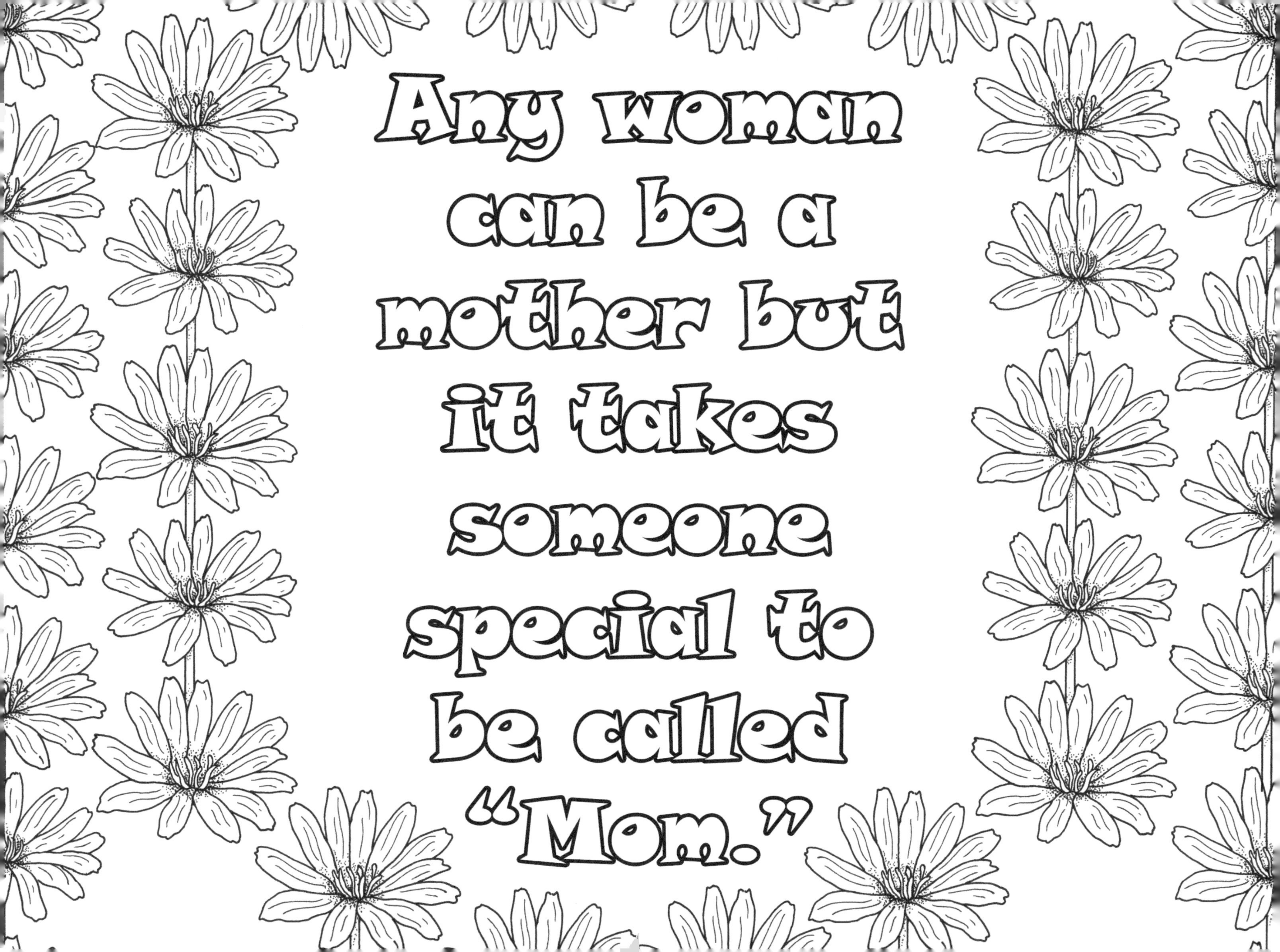
Any woman can be a mother but it takes someone special to be called "Mom."

There is no replacement for you.

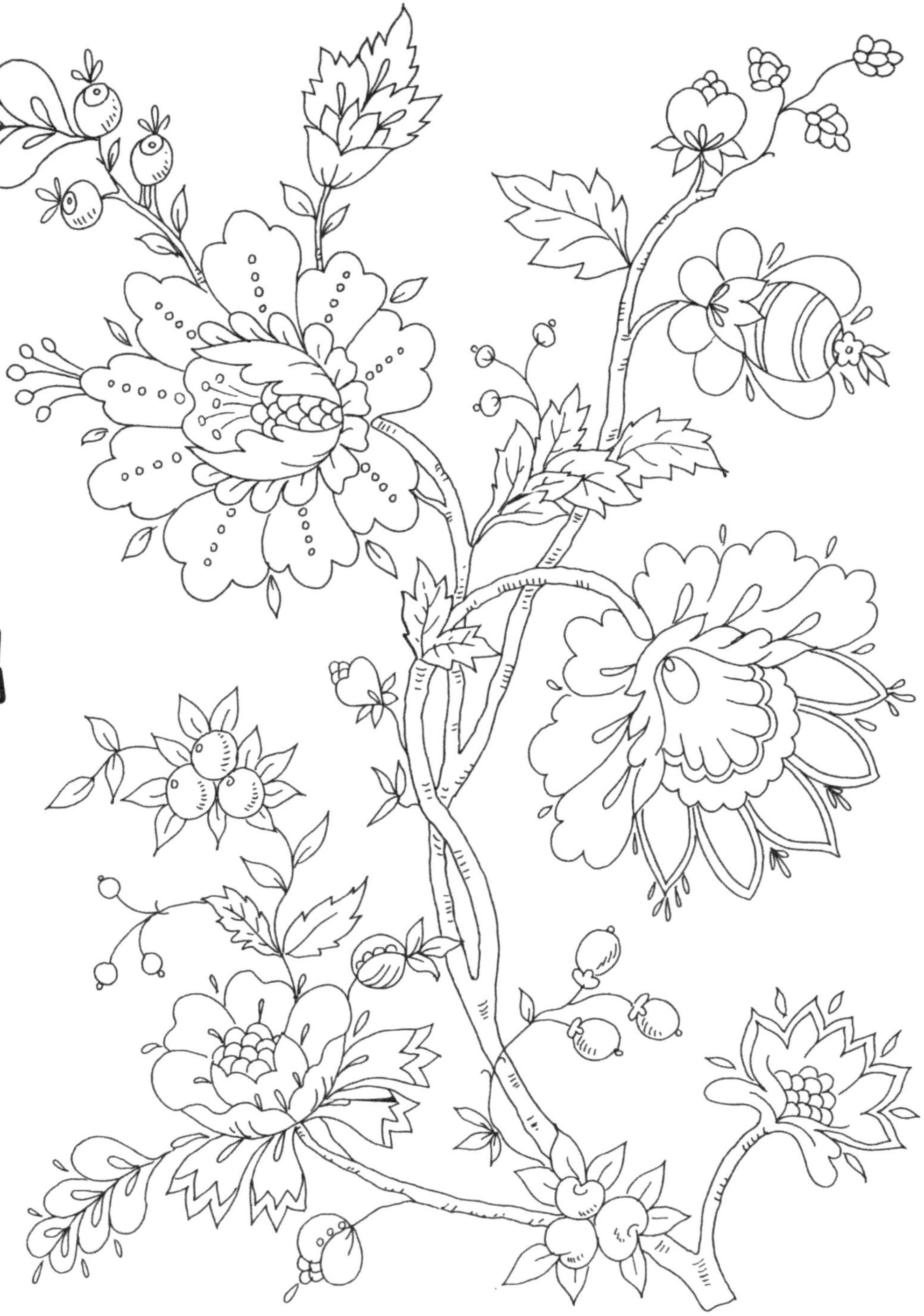

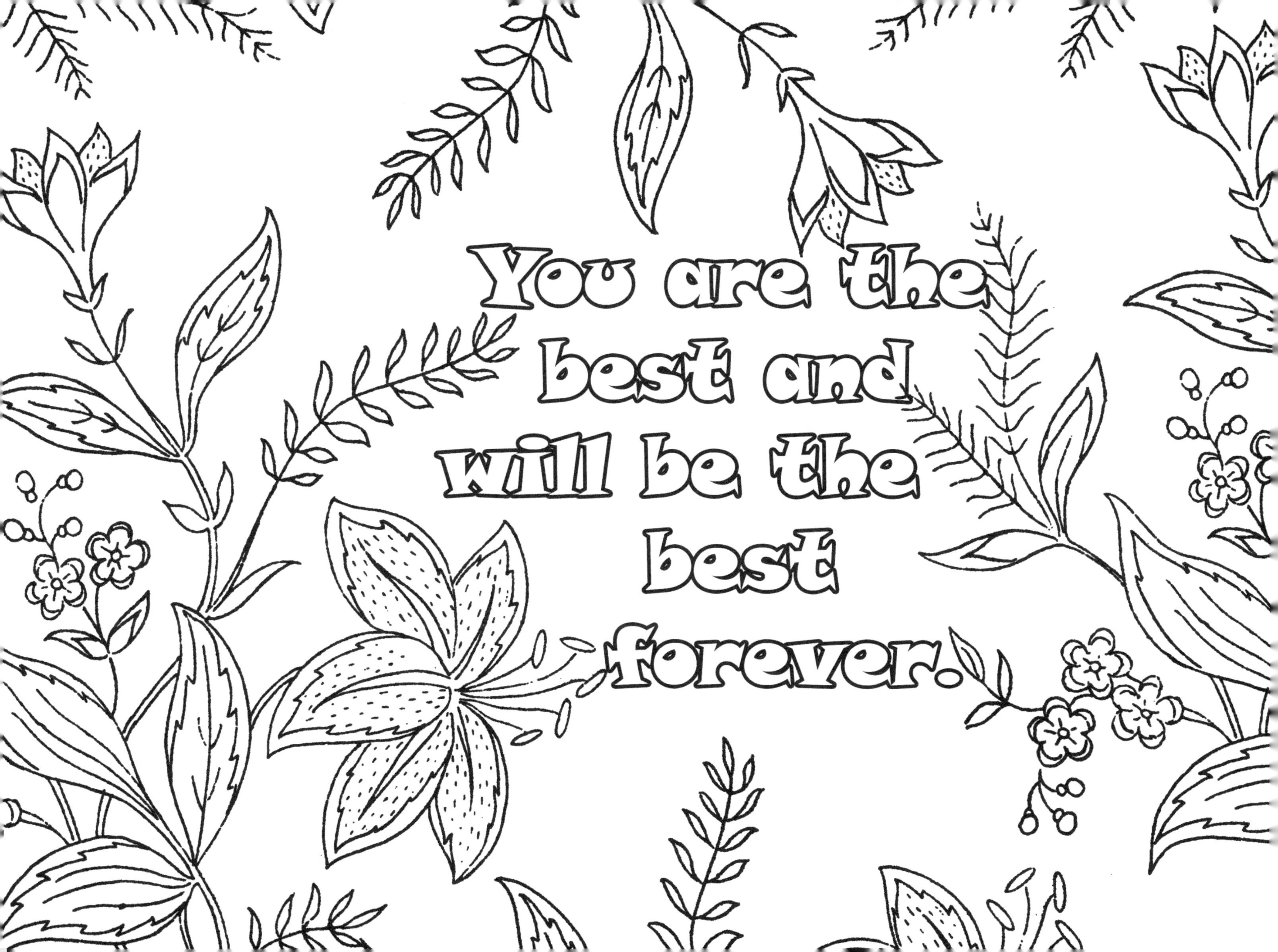
You are the best and will be the best forever.

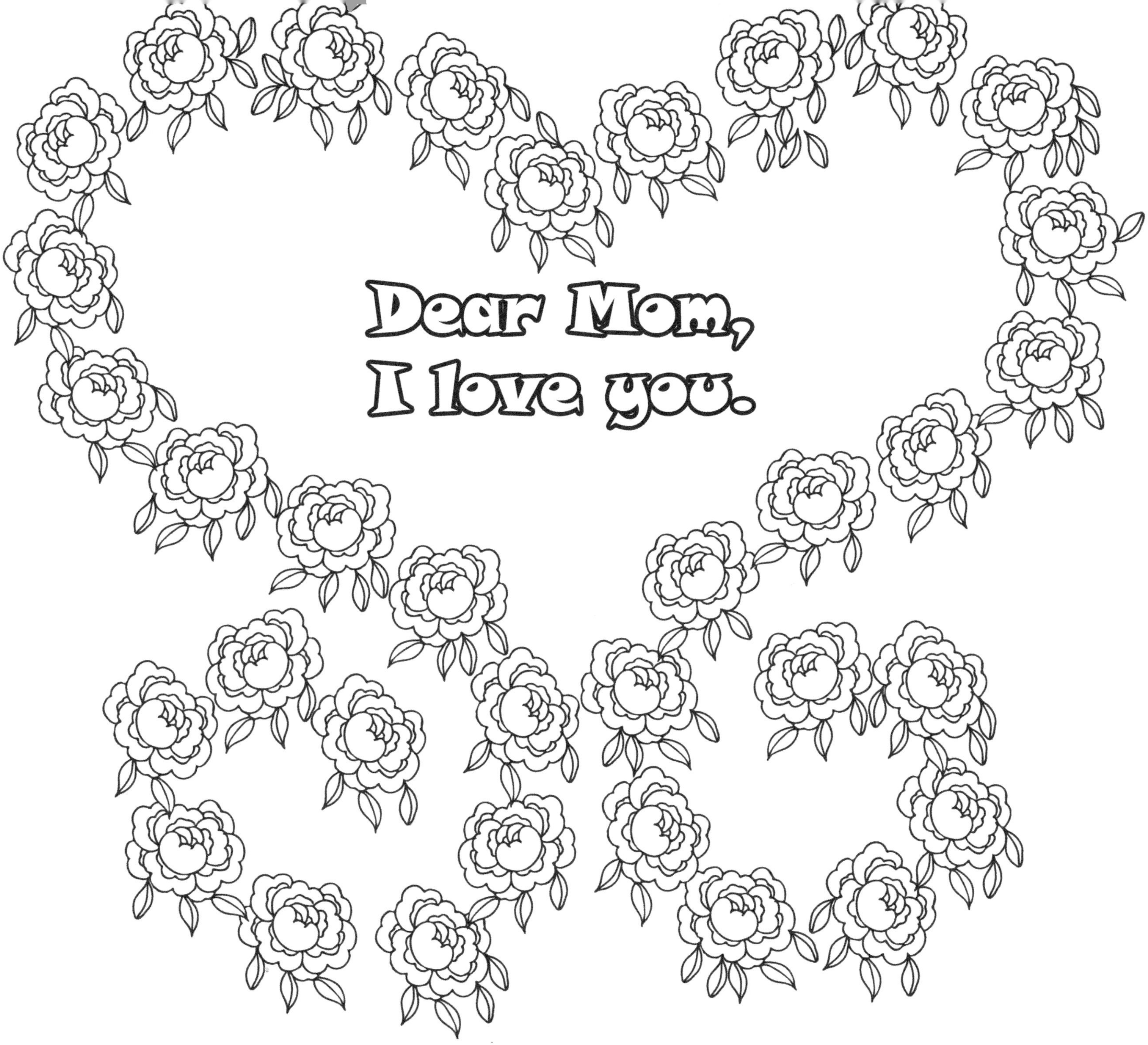
Dear Mom,
I love you.

www.ingramcontent.com/pod-product-compliance
Lightning Source LLC
Chambersburg PA
CBHW080024110526
44587CB00022BA/3948
* 9 7 8 1 7 1 3 9 0 1 6 7 9 *